Advance Praise for
Europeans in Hong Kong

"Hong Kong has always been a cosmopolitan city. Mark O'Neill's book marvellously highlights how much, not only the British, but also the other Europeans, as the German, the French and the Portuguese, have played a dynamic role in making Hong Kong successful, both before and after the metropolis' handover to China in 1997."
— Jean-Pierre Cabestan, Emeritus Professor of Political Science, Hong Kong Baptist University

"That Hong Kong is a Chinese city is no more contestable than the fact that it is now part of China. But the contribution of other people to the making of this most remarkable of places is easily overlooked. Mark O'Neill restores the balance with this highly readable account of the numerous continental Europeans who, from the earliest times to the present day came to live, work and contribute to Hong Kong. Warm, engaging and sympathetic, *Europeans in Hong Kong* is a welcome antidote to the narrow 'nationalistic' narratives that obscure whatever is thought to be politically inconvenient when it comes to explaining the past."
— Graham Hutchings, Associate, University of Oxford China Centre

"The publication by Mark O'Neill titled "The Europeans of Hong Kong" is a valuable source of information on Hong Kong and its history. Through deep research and multiple contacts, the book collects information on European communities in town and shows the positive contribution offered to the economic development of the metropolis as a modern finance and trade center. The Italian presence has been growing over the years with a significant number of Italian nationals initially mainly linked to religious Organizations such as PIME and the Canossian sisters, which are still a widely acknowledged and integral feature in the social structure of the city. Thanks to the contribution of Italian citizens who have established in Hong Kong their permanent residency over time and are now perfectly integrated in various sectors of the local economic and social environment, nowadays Italy has expanded its interest in multiple fields such as culture, art, business, lifestyle and sport, and it is considered as source of inspiration by many locals."

—Italian Consul-General Carmelo Ficarra

To Graham

EUROPEANS IN HONG KONG

With thanks and best wishes
Mark
Leamington Spa
27. vi. 2025

MARK O'NEILL

Europeans in Hong Kong

By Mark O'Neill

Trade Paper: 978-988-8904-23-5
Digital: 978-988-8904-22-8

© 2025 Mark O'Neill

HISTORY / Asia / Hong Kong

EB230

All rights reserved. No part of this book may be reproduced in material form, by any means, whether graphic, electronic, mechanical or other, including photocopying or information storage, in whole or in part. May not be used to prepare other publications without written permission from the publisher except in the case of brief quotations embodied in critical articles or reviews. For information contact info@earnshawbooks.com

Published in Hong Kong by Earnshaw Books Ltd.

Table of Contents

Introduction	vii
Chapter One – The Germans	1
Chapter Two – The French	53
Chapter Three – The Italians	125
Chapter Four – The Portuguese	157
Chapter Five – The Spanish	187
Chapter Six – Two Individuals	208
Conclusion	219
Sources	221
Thanks and Acknowledgements	225

Introduction

Hong Kong is the most European city in Asia. It is full of churches, schools, hospitals and institutions built by Europeans that have become part of the fabric of the city. Tens of thousands of Europeans have made their home here and live here even today.

This book is about those who came to Hong Kong from the European continent. The British and the Irish have also made great contributions, of course. Britain was the colonial power that created the city we see today and managed it until 1997. Ireland won its independence from London in 1922; it was the first colony to leave the British Empire. Before and after 1922, Irish people played an important role here as administrators, soldiers, policemen, judges, lawyers, doctors, teachers, missionaries, bankers, entrepreneurs and jockeys. The British and the Irish both deserve separate volumes on their histories in Hong Kong. But this book has a different subject — citizens of the five EU countries who have made the greatest contribution – France, Germany, Portugal, Spain and Italy. And we have added Hungarian Jesuit priest Laszlo Ladany, the world's top China-watcher for thirty years, and Anders Nelsson, the Swedish singer and long-term Hong Kong resident well-known to local residents. Other Europeans we had to exclude because of lack of space; to them, we apologize.

The aim of this book is to describe the great European contribution to Hong Kong. Most people believe that Hong Kong

EUROPEANS IN HONG KONG

was built by Chinese during 150 years of British rule, which is not entirely accurate. As the reader will discover, many of the city's schools, hospitals, welfare institutions, buildings and businesses were founded and run by people from Europe (defined here as 'east of Calais'). Many lived here for their entire adult and returned "home" only when forced to by war or ill health. Visit the city's cemeteries and you will find traces of many of them. They became more fond of the city and its people than of their mother country. The European presence grew after 1949. The new government in China closed the door to foreigners, except for people from a small number from other Socialist countries. Wishing to stay in China and the Chinese world, many Europeans moved from the Mainland to Hong Kong. They brought with them their businesses, churches, schools and hospitals. For the next 30 years, it was the only place where foreigners could do business with China. After Deng Xiaoping re-opened the country's doors in 1980, they could live in Beijing, Shanghai and other Mainland cities. But many chose, and still choose, to live in Hong Kong because they like the city so much, even if most of the goods they make, use and trade are manufactured in the Mainland. Many stay on after they retire from full-time employment. Some divide their time between Hong Kong, their home country and perhaps other places, but they have too many friends and connections here to leave.

Immediately after the British established the colony in 1841, people from continental Europe started to arrive, and they have never stopped coming, except during the two World Wars. Today, more than 50,000 citizens of the 27 countries of the European Union live here; 16 have consulates-general in Hong Kong. Many have more nationals living here than in any other city in Asia. The inflow rose strongly from the early 1990s, partly because of the collapse of communism in Eastern Europe, which opened the way for citizens of those countries to move here. And the growth has continued since the handover in 1997.

Europeans are active in all sectors of life. They are businessmen, traders and in finance: architects, doctors, vets, engineers, priests, musicians, artists, journalists, photographers, volunteers and active in conservation. They run restaurants, boutiques and art galleries: they make films and advertisements; they import and export wine and gourmet food: they run high-tech companies; they help refugees, the poor and the elderly. They have become part of the fiber of the city. Of European residents, the French rank first with 25,000, followed at a distance by the Germans with 4,000. More than 800 French companies are represented in Hong Kong; 600 German companies have offices here — half of them headquarters for the Asia-Pacific region.

During the first eighty years of Hong Kong's existence from the early 1840s, many of the European arrivals were religious, Catholic and Protestant. They built schools, hospitals and churches and cared for children, the sick, the poor and the elderly. Without them, tens of thousands of Chinese children, especially girls, would have died. Other early arrivals were business people; they managed shipping, trading and financial companies and moved goods between Europe and China. They helped to make Hong Kong one of the most important ports and commercial centers of East Asia in the 19th century. Everyone came to take advantage of the legal and political protection provided by the colonial government. Hong Kong offered people personal and professional opportunities they could not find at home, as well as a higher quality of living, lower taxes and escape from the bitter European winter.

These harmonious exchanges were rudely interrupted by the two World Wars. Before 1914, the Germans were the most important business community after the British, and well

EUROPEANS IN HONG KONG

integrated into expatriate society. After the declaration of war in August 1914, German residents here were interned and their businesses confiscated; by 1921, there were only three Germans left in the city. The Japanese occupation between December 1941 and August 1945 caused a similar upheaval. Citizens of Allied nations were interned and the Japanese took control of the economy. Travel between Europe and Hong Kong became impossible.

With the rapid growth of Hong Kong from the 1950s, migration from Europe resumed. European companies were eager to take part in the city's large construction projects and export its goods around the world. The opening of China after 1979 provided a further stimulus. Hong Kong became a financial, shipping, retail and services center for all of China. European companies and individuals poured in to seize the chance. Since the 1980s, the number of Europeans living here has greatly increased. They have been attracted by Hong Kong's economic opportunities, generous visa policy, low taxes, good living environment and religious and cultural tolerance. They enjoy the high quality of service, excellent medical care and public transport, good law and order and the wide use of English. People who live here for seven consecutive years can apply for permanent residence, a right offered by few countries in Asia.

Hong Kong people have greatly benefitted from this European presence. It has given them opportunities not available in any other city in China. Tens of thousands of Hong Kong people have attended schools and hospitals established by European religious orders. They work in European banks, companies and institutions. They have personal and professional opportunities to study, live and work abroad. Europeans run schools, language institutes, film festivals, music and cultural events. Hong Kong people can learn French at the Alliance Francaise, German at the

Goethe Institut and Spanish at the Spanish Cultural Association. They can send their children to the French International School, German-Swiss International School, Spanish Primary School and Norwegian International School. They can attend festivals of European films, theater, music and exhibitions, for a firsthand experience of the continent's rich culture. They can also taste its varied cuisine, thanks to all ther European chefs working in major hotels or running their own restaurants. They can buy the latest European products, from luxury handbags and jewelry to fashion, wine and cheese. Through the consulates, cultural institutes, chambers of commerce and exchange associations, Hong Kong people can earn scholarships and job placements in universities and companies in Europe. They have a window open to Europe and Europeans that few other cities in Asia offer.

Before the fall of the Berlin Wall in 1989, it was difficult, if not impossible, for citizens of the Soviet Union and its satellite countries in Eastern Europe to live and work in Hong Kong. That changed after the collapse of communism in Europe; nine countries in Eastern Europe joined the EU. Poland, Lithuania and Romania have their own Chambers of Commerce. Polish Catholics can hear Mass in their own language at the Notre Dame Chapel in Ma Tau Wai in Kowloon. In 1996, the Orthodox Metropolitanate of Hong Kong was founded, after a decision of the Ecumenical Patriarchate of Constantinople. Members of the Orthodox Church can attend services at the Orthodox Cathedral of Saint Luke in the Universal Trade Center in Arbuthnot Road, Central.

Economically, the EU is very important for Hong Kong. In 2023, Hong Kong was the EU's 31st largest trading partner in goods. The EU is Hong Kong›s third-largest trade partner after Mainland China and Taiwan. In commercial services, Hong Kong ranked in 2022 as the EU's tenth-biggest trading partner, double the level of 2017. The main areas of EU-Hong Kong trade in services are transportation, and business and financial services.

By the end of 2022, EU firms had invested a total of €96 billion in Hong Kong, while Hong Kong companies had invested €194 billion in the EU, most of that reflecting Hong Kong's role as a waystation for China funds. According to statistics from Hong Kong, the EU was in 2022 the fifth largest investor in Hong Kong and the second destination for Hong Kong's FDI globally. As of 2023, the EU was the largest foreign business community in Hong Kong, according to a survey carried out by the Hong Kong SAR government. A total of 1,548 EU companies have businesses in Hong Kong and about half of them use Hong Kong as their regional headquarters or regional offices. The EU's business presence covers a large variety of sectors, including financial and business services, trading, logistics, construction, and retailing. EU companies are key players in a range of sectors of the Hong Kong economy, including banking, insurance, securities, logistics and infrastructure.

Since 2005, the Special Administrative Region (SAR) government and the European Union (EU) have held a high-level annual meeting called the Structured Dialogue, to maintain close contacts and develop positive relations. The SAR government has Economic and Trade Offices in Brussels, headquarters of the EU, and in Berlin. In Hong Kong, there is a European Chamber of Commerce, as well as 14 national chambers of commerce. Going the other way, Hong Kong is among the top six foreign investors in the EU.

For nearly two centuries, then, the ties between Europe and Hong Kong have been deep and of benefit to both sides. They have covered all sectors of society, from churches, schools and hospitals to trade and commerce and from sport and fast cars to music, cinema and fine food. Hong Kong has given tens of

MARK O'NEILL

thousands of Europeans an excellent place to work, develop and prosper. Their presence has provided similar opportunities for Hong Kong and opened doors for them to work, study and settle in Europe. Let us hope this rich relationship continues for decades to come.

Chapter One
The Germans

Business First

The establishment of a British colony in Hong Kong presented an opportunity to many in Europe, allowing them to take advantage of the political stability and legal system provided by British rule. First to come were religious orders; they saw the city as a base to evangelize China and other countries in Asia. They came from France, Italy, Spain and Germany. Next were business people, who saw the benefits of Hong Kong's excellent harbor and its position as a center to trade goods between Europe and Asia, especially China. For the first seventy-five years of Hong Kong's history, the Germans were the most important business community after the British. This chapter will describe their substantial presence here—until it was dramatically shut down by World War I.

In commerce, the Germans were the quickest of the Europeans to move. Their banks, trading firms and business people seized the opportunities offered by this unique open port on the coast of China. By 1877, the city had twenty-one German wholesale trade companies, five agents for money exchange,

EUROPEANS IN HONG KONG

shipping and securities and eight shops. When the Hong Kong General Chamber of Commerce was founded in 1861, a German, D. Nissen, was elected onto the board. Four Germans served as board members of the Hongkong & Shanghai Banking Corporation (HSBC), and three Germans sat on the seven-person board of the Hong Kong & Whampoa Dock Company.

In 1864, Michael Jebsen visited Hong Kong as captain of the barque *Notos* and saw the need for steamships to replace sailing vessels. So he set up his own fleet; it had fourteen steamers with German masters and Chinese crew, transporting goods and passengers along the China coast. On March 1, 1895, his two sons, Jacob and Heinrich, founded Jebsen & Co in Hong Kong. It is flourishing one hundred and twenty-eight years later and is one of the city's oldest European trading firms. It remains today a family company, headed by Hans Michael Jebsen (捷成漢), the grandson of the founder.

In the first fifty years after 1841, Germans invested at least 20 million Deutschmarks into seven of Hong Kong's biggest companies. In 1898, seventeen per cent of all ships entering Hong Kong harbor sailed under the German flag, second to Britain with forty-three per cent and ahead of eleven per cent for Japan and eight per cent from the United States. A report by the German consulate in 1907 for the Chancellor in Berlin said that sixty per cent of total imports from Europe to Hong Kong and sixty-five per cent of total exports from Hong Kong to Europe passed through German hands. It said that the city had thirty-eight German firms and, on average, one third of the board members of important British companies were German.

This economic importance was far out of proportion to the numbers—in January 1897, there were only 208 Germans, out of 3,625 Europeans and Americans. There were 2,267 Portuguese, mainly from Macao; 1,349 Indians: Parsees and other nationalities

969; and Eurasians 272. Among the German community, in addition to those in trade and banking, were missionaries, doctors, watchmakers, auctioneers, insurance and shipping agents, those running bars, cafes, hostels and restaurants, shopkeepers, tobacconists and a gunsmith. By 1911, the number had risen to 342. The community could attend church services in German and see doctors from their own country. In 1853, German doctors opened a Medical Hall in Queens Road, to serve the needs of their community and others who chose to consult them. It had German pharmacists as well as doctors. It continued to operate until 1914, when it was liquidated after the outbreak of World War I. In 1873, German merchants founded the first German Protestant congregation in Hong Kong and elected Ernst Klitzke as pastor. He had arrived in the city in May 1867 as pastor and director of the Bethesda, a German orphanage (described below). He raised money from German and British companies to build a chapel next to Bethesda; it opened on March 14, 1881. Exhausted, he died of heart failure on July 3 that year and is buried in Happy Valley Cemetery.

This strong German presence was due to two factors. In 1871, Otto von Bismarck unified the country and created the German empire. This unification and the industrial-oriented policies of Bismarck and successive governments led to the fast rise of the German economy. The country was a latecomer in this respect compared to Britain, Belgium, the Netherlands and France. By the first decennia of the 20th Century, Germany had overtaken Britain in industrial production, first in output of steel and chemicals, and became second in the world after the US. This naturally affected her status in Hong Kong where Germans had a strong position in certain industries and services. German trading firms in Hong Kong sold their country's industrial products to China, including machinery, armaments and munitions.

EUROPEANS IN HONG KONG

The other factor was the attractiveness of Hong Kong as a free port that offered equal treatment to foreign companies and good access to markets in China and other countries in the Far East. Like other nationalities who moved to the city, Germans could live and work as they wished; they could attend their own places of worship and establish their own clubs and social networks. With the low cost of domestic help, they could enjoy a standard of living impossible at home. Starting from 1848, many German companies set up offices in the city, to take advantage of the economic boom in their home country and the large profit margins from trading. Between 1880 and 1913, Britain's share of world trade had declined from 38.2 percent to 30.2 percent; Germany's share increased from 17.2 percent to 26.6 percent. Between 1890 and 1913, German exports tripled; by 1913, its share of world manufacturing production was 14.8 percent, overtaking Britain with 13.6 percent.

A symbol of this economic and social power was the Club Germania. It was founded in a modest building in Wanchai in 1859. In 1865, it moved to larger premises; but that proved to be too small. So in 1872 it moved to a new building on the east side of Wyndham Street and Queen's Road. It was a building in the Gothic style that cost HK$21,000 and had thirteen granite steps to the entrance and main hall. It had a library, reading room, billiard room, bowling alley, bar, and dining hall. It hosted concerts, lectures and German VIPS visiting the city. It was essential for the exchange of news and opinion and for new arrivals who needed an orientation from their fellow countrymen. It created a sense of collective identity. The concert hall could accommodate 275 people and the dining room sixty. During the Franco-German war of 1870 and 1871, the German community collected large sums of money and sent to care for the sick and wounded. At a single concert in December in 1870, they raised HK$2,000.

MARK O'NEILL

This building in Central also became too small; so, in 1902, the club moved to a new one at 7 Kennedy Road, an imposing structure with five storys looking over Victoria Harbor. In 1914, the government seized it as enemy property. In September 1918, it became the property of St Joseph's College (聖若瑟書院); the school continues to use the building to this day.

One of the leading lights of the Club was Baron Gustav Von Overbeck. Born in March 1830 in the west of Germany, he emigrated to the US and became a whaler in the Bering Sea, based in Honolulu. In the late 1850s, he moved to Hong Kong and began work with Dent & Co, a British trading firm. He was a trustee of the Bethesda Orphanage, which we will describe below; its premises on High Street, Sai Ying Poon, were built on land he bought in 1859. He constructed the second building of Club Germania at the top of Wyndham Street in 1865. He was one of the main investors in the Hongkong Hotel, which opened on February 29, 1868. In the late 1870s, he purchased a concession in Northern Borneo that includes most of present-day Sabah. In December 1877, he was made Maharajah of Sabah. He had two families. One was with an American wife with whom he had three sons. The other was with a Chinese lady in Hong

Kong, with whom he had four daughters. He died in London in April 1894.

Dr Ferdinand Korn was a German hired by the Butterfield & Swire Company as the first general manager and chief chemist of the sugar plant it built in 1881. Born in Wiesbaden in 1853, he studied chemistry in Heidelberg and then Dresden, where he received a doctorate in organic chemistry at the age of twenty-one. At that time, chemistry was a very modern discipline. He worked as a research assistant in Dresden, specializing in the chemistry of sugar and its industrial production. In 1881, Butterfield & Swire recruited him to come to Hong Kong and run their sugar plant. Construction of the Tai Koo Sugar Refinery took three years and cost £200,000, with an additional £500,000 invested over the next ten years. It purchased raw sugar from Java and the Philippines and produced a wide range of sugar products, including white and powdered sugar. Production began in 1884/85, with output of 700 metric tonnes per week. Its market strategy was to supply and stimulate demand for white sugar in Asia. It sold refined sugar products to China, Japan, Australia, India and California. Dr Korn was a skilled chemist who improved the quality of the products; he managed the factory for ten years. His son Ferdinand was born in Hong Kong in 1892, but his wife died here of tuberculosis. Other Germans followed him into the factory. Between 1884 and 1900, it generated profits and dividends totaling £1 million. By the 1920s, it was the largest single refinery in the world. Butterfield & Swire built a company town, with housing for Chinese workers and their families, schools, recreational facilities and a 200-meter cable car to take Dr Korn and the other European managers to their homes up the mountain.

Dr Korn left Hong Kong a rich man; some of his wealth was in the form of shares in the Swire Company. During World War

I, however, the government expropriated these shares as 'enemy property'. He is remembered today in Kornhill and Kornhill Gardens (康怡花園), an apartment complex built on the site of where he and other senior managers lived. Tai Koo Place occupies the land where the refinery stood. The memory of the refinery lives on in Tong Chong Street (糖廠街), which means the 'Street of the Sugar Factory'.

Jebsen & Co was a good example of German enterprise in Hong Kong. It was founded on March 1, 1895, by Jacob Jebsen and Heinrich Jessen; they were relatives from the same town, Apenrade, in the Duchy of Schleswig in Germany. The town was part of Denmark until 1864; its Danish name is Aabenraa. Jacob's father Michael operated a fleet of merchant steamships in European and East Asian waters. He first visited Hong Kong in 1864 as captain of the barque Notos and saw the need for steamships to replace sailing vessels and set up his own fleet. He was a figure of national importance—a member of the Prussian Diet and the German Parliament. The two partners chose as the company logo a laurel wreath surrounding three mackerel, the heraldic shield of Aabenraa; the fish have a large appetite and are fast and nimble swimmers. The town has Denmark's seventh largest harbor. For a century from 1750, it had the third largest trading fleet of the Danish monarchy, as well as shipbuilding yards. The most famous of its ships was the clipper Cimber, which sailed from Liverpool to San Francisco in 106 days. The two founders of Jebsen & Co grew up immersed in this rich maritime tradition. In 1864, the town became part of Prussia and, in 1871, part of Germany.

The new firm was funded by 20,000 Deutschmarks, half from Michael Jebsen and half from Jessen, with a further loan 20,000 Deutschmarks from family friends. It began as agents for Michael Jebsen's fleet and expanded this shipping service to an agency for the Shanghai-Tsingtao Mail Line. In 1896, the firm joined the Hong Kong General Chamber of Commerce. In 1897, it signed an agreement with Baden Aniline and Soda Factory (BASF) to trade indigo dye, its debut in the industrial sector; BASF went on to be an important customer for 84 years. In 1898, it set up its first joint venture in China, which included a brick factory in Qingdao. With the growth in business, in October 1906, it moved to large premises in Connaught Road Central; it also opened a branch office and warehouse in Shameen, in Guangzhou in 1907. In 1906, it acquired Blue Girl Beer (藍妹啤酒); this turned out to be a smart investment—more than 110 years later, it has about 20 percent of the Hong Kong beer market, the most popular brand. It became an important player in China trade; its products included Bolinder engines, scrap metal, rubber waste, hog bristles, duck feathers, ginger, tungsten, antimony and rattan. It never traded opium. In the spring of 1914, the firm's balance sheets showed a cumulative capital of 5 million Deutschmarks in its first twenty years, with most of the profits coming from goods, rather than shipping.

The new firm was funded by 20,000 Deutschmarks, half from Michael Jebsen and half from Jessen, with a further loan 20,000 Deutschmarks from family friends. It began as agents for Michael Jebsen's fleet and expanded this shipping service to an agency for the Shanghai-Tsingtao Mail Line. In 1896, the firm joined the Hong Kong General Chamber of Commerce. In 1897, it signed an agreement with Baden Aniline and Soda Factory (BASF) to trade indigo dye, its debut in the industrial sector; BASF went on to be an important customer for 84 years. In 1898, it set up its first joint venture in China, which included a brick factory in Qingdao. With the growth in business, in October 1906, it moved to large premises in Connaught Road Central; it also opened a branch office and warehouse in Shameen, in Guangzhou in 1907.

In 1906, it acquired Blue Girl Beer (藍妹啤酒); this turned out to be a smart investment—more than 110 years later, it has about 20 percent of the Hong Kong beer market, the most popular brand. It became an important player in China trade; its products included Bolinder engines, scrap metal, rubber waste, hog bristles, duck feathers, ginger, tungsten, antimony and rattan. It never traded opium. In the spring of 1914, the firm's balance sheets showed a cumulative capital of 5 million Deutschmarks in its first twenty years, with most of the profits coming from goods, rather than shipping.

Not all the Germans in Hong Kong worked in business and commerce. Wilhelm Lobscheid was the first German to serve as Inspector of Government Schools, from 1857 to 1859. He was born on March 19, 1822, in a village east of the River Rhine. A missionary society sent him to Hong Kong, where he arrived on May 22 1848. Working under Charles Gutzlaff, he founded a school to train Chinese Christians as missionaries. He was fluent in Cantonese and Mandarin and wrote more than twenty-five books on religion, education and linguistics, mostly in Chinese and English and a few in German. From 1866 to 1869, he produced a four-volume English and Chinese Dictionary. He was an active Inspector of Government Schools, promoting new secular subjects and improving the quality of teachers. He left China in 1870 and settled as a doctor in the United States; he died there on Christmas Day 1890.

The second German inspector of schools was Ernst Johann Eitel, who held the post from 1879 to 1896. He was born on February 13, 1838, in Wurttemberg. He was educated at the Theological Seminary of Schontal and Tubingen University, when he obtained an MA in 1860. After serving as a vicar for one year, he joined the Basel Mission to China. This society was based in Basel, Switzerland, and recruited most of its missionaries from

EUROPEANS IN HONG KONG

Wurttemberg in southern Germany. It sent Eitel to Guangzhou in 1860 as a missionary. He learnt Hakka (客家話) and Cantonese (廣東話). He arrived in Hong Kong in 1862. In 1865, he joined the London Missionary Society, which gave him permission to marry Mary Eaton, Lady Superintendent of the Diocesan Native Female Training School, now the Diocesan Girls' School, in 1866. The couple spent the next four years in Boluo County (博羅縣) in eastern Guangdong; they moved back to Hong Kong in 1870. Eitel was an accomplished scholar and linguist; he wrote widely, including articles and the Chinese Dictionary of the Cantonese Dialect in 1877. He was appointed Inspector of Schools. He chaired a committee of school textbooks and supervised the studies of government officers learning Cantonese. As school inspector, he promoted female education, early childhood and physical education and industrial training; he also introduced standardized examinations using British models. One of Eitel's most important legacies was the foundation in 1890 of the Central School for Girls; it was the first government school for young ladies in the city and offered education in both English and Chinese. In 1893, it accepted a donation of HK$25,000 from Emanuel Belilos, a Jewish entrepreneur and philanthropist, and was renamed Belilos Public School (庇理羅士女子中學).The school stands today in Tin Hau Temple Road, where it moved in April 1965. With 850 students, it has been one of the most prestigious secondary schools in Hong Kong, with English as its principal medium of instruction.

Eitel was an accomplished author. He wrote a detailed account of the first forty years of the city, *Europe in China: the History of Hongkong from the Beginning to the year 1882*, published by Kelly and Walsh in 1895. The book was carefully sourced and gave a proper role to Chinese community leaders in the city's early development. It is very detailed, a tribute to the author's hard work, reading of contemporary newspapers and his own knowledge of the city. He also used material from official documents, which were later lost or destroyed during the Japanese occupation from 1941/45. This is from the preface: "by fifty years' handling of Hongkong's Chinese population, Great Britain has shewn how readily the Chinese people (apart from Mandarindom) fall in with a firm European regime, and the rapid conversion of a barren rock into one of the wonders and commercial emporiums of the world, has demonstrated what Chinese labor, industry and commerce can achieve under British rule." Ever since, his book has been an invaluable history for scholars of Hong Kong. He wrote at least eight other books, on subjects including Buddhism, feng-shui and "*A Chinese Dictionary in the Cantonese Dialect*". Eitel retired in 1896, with a government pension of HK$1,620 a year, and went to live with his wife and four children in Adelaide. He became minister of St Stephen's Lutheran Church and lecturer in German Language and Literature at the University of Adelaide. He died in the city on November 10, 1908. He and Lobscheid were among the very small number of Germans serving in the government. The rest of the community was happy to concentrate on business and stay out of politics.

Missionaries
In the 1841-1918 period, there were German missionaries also, but not as many as those from France and Italy. They have also left a legacy in Hong Kong that survives today. Karl Friedrich August Gutzlaff, also known as Charles Gutzlaff, was a pioneer missionary and polyglot and one of the earliest Germans in Hong Kong. He was born in Pomerania, Prussia on July 8, 1803, and sent by the Netherlands Missionary Society in 1827 to Sumatra. There he began a study of written and spoken Chinese, including

EUROPEANS IN HONG KONG

Mandarin, Fujianese and Cantonese. In 1831, he took a ship for Tianjin and handed out Christian tracts on the way. He worked as an interpreter for Charles Elliott during the first Opium War (1840-42) and for Sir Henry Pottinger, the first Governor of Hong Kong. From 1842 to his death in August 1851, he served as chief secretary to the Superintendent of Trade and Governor of Hong Kong. His translations of Christian literature were widely used by the Taiping rebels; it was led by Hong Xiuquan (洪秀全), who believed he was the brother of Jesus Christ. Between 1850 and 1864, the Taiping controlled a large area of southern China, with a population of thirty million; their aim was to overthrow the Qing dynasty and create a new social and moral order which they called Taiping Heavenly Kingdom (太平天國). With military support from the Western powers, the Qing defeated the rebellion. Estimates of the dead range between twenty and thirty million soldiers and civilians, killed in the fighting, famine and disease.

One legacy of German missionaries is the Ebenezer School and Home for the Visually Impaired (心光盲人院暨學校) on 131 Pokfulam Road. It was founded in 1897 by Hildesheimer Blindenmission (HBM, Hildesheimer Mission for the Blind). This was a charity set up seven years before in the town of that name, thirty kilometers southeast of Hanover in northern Germany; its mission was to spread the gospel and take care of and train blind girls. It sent missionary Martha Postler to Hong Kong. Her first site was in Western, where she accepted four girls. In 1901, Ebenezer was granted a site in To Kwa Wan to build a hostel for fifty blind girls. The home taught them braille, knitting, straw-weaving and other occupations. In 1911, the government granted the current site at 131 Pokfulam Road. During World War I, the Church Missionary Society took over the home, but the sisters in charge were allowed to continue to care for the children; in

1928, the To Kwa Wan home was returned to HBM. In 1930, the Pokfulam Home reopened and all the children moved there. During World War II, the government took over the building and the girls did not return until 1948. Initially, financial support for Ebenezer came entirely from the HBM and private donations in Hong Kong and abroad. In 1954, it received its first subvention from the Social Welfare Department and the Education Bureau in Hong Kong to maintain existing and new programs. It is also a member of the Community Chest, and receives support from the Hong Kong Jockey Club and private donations. It remains today one of the only schools in Hong Kong dedicated to students with visual impairment. Today it includes not only blind girls, but also male students, elderly people with visual impairments and students with multiple disabilities. It has a department called Project WORKS, which finds employment and internship opportunities for the blind in Hong Kong.

The Lutheran Kau Yan Church (救恩堂, Saving Grace Church) in Sai Ying Poon (西營盤) is another legacy of a German missionary; its address is 97A High St, Sai Wan. Rudolph Lechler (黎力基) of the Basel Missionary Society arrived in Hong Kong in early 1847, aged 22, and lived in China for fifty-two years, He started his missionary work in rural communities of Guangdong Province, especially among the Hakka community. The Kau Yun Church, built with HK$1,800 he raised, opened in 1863. In 1874, he became head of the Basel Missionary Society in China. He was responsible for the mission to the Hakka people, which established fifty-one mission stations and fifty-six schools. The mission helped communities fleeing from persecution in the Mainland to resettle in Southeast Asia. Lechler was able to preach in Mandarin, Fujianese and Hakka. He helped to prepare a romanized Hakka edition of the Gospels of Matthew and Luke. His final work after returning to Germany in 1899 was to compile a Hakka dictionary. The first Chinese pastor was appointed in 1878. After 1949, the church opened a primary and secondary school. With many of the Hakka residents moving to other parts of Hong Kong, the church offered morning services in Hakka and afternoon ones in Cantonese. In 1985, the congregation had 923 members, including 202 children.

Another German missionary initiative, which has not survived, was the Orphanage Bethesda. It was set up in 1861 by the Berlin Women's Missionary Society for China, to receive female babies and girls abandoned by their families. This was due to the Chinese custom of regarding male children as more prestigious and economically useful than female ones. To save these girls from death was a great humanitarian deed by the Sisters. The Orphanage was a spacious colonial building that offered a home for over 100 girls in a world that did not welcome them. Most were found by traveling missionaries in southern China, abandoned or left on the road to die, and brought to Hong Kong. The orphanage provided them with a modern education, with the aim of raising 'good Christian housewives' and marrying them to good Christian Chinese husbands. Some became nurses, teachers or even doctors. After they left, they kept a close relation to the orphanage that had rescued them and given them a chance in life. In 1880, the orphanage built a small church next door; it was the first German Evangelical Church in Hong Kong. During its history of more than fifty years, more than 1,000 girls passed through the institution. It gave them a home, a family and training. This upbringing made them more self-reliant and better educated than the average Chinese girl. The funding for the institution came from private donations in Germany and Hong Kong. In World War I, it was shut down as enemy property; it did not reopen after the war. Instead, Hong Kong residents came to the orphanage, inspected the girls and chose them as domestic helpers or possible daughters-in-law.

World War One

The Germans in Hong Kong lived and worked in harmony with the British community. They had similar working practises, lifestyles and religious beliefs. One of the most important British officials of this period was Sir Francis May. From 1893 to 1902, he was Chief of Police and Colonial Secretary from 1902 to 1910; he became Governor in July 1912. He was pro-German and a friend of German consul Arthur Voretzsch. But, while there was harmony in Hong Kong, there was from 1900 growing military and political rivalry in Europe between Britain and Germany. War seemed inevitable. Bert Becker, an associate professor of history at the University of Hong Kong, found a telegram sent by May to Voretzsch on August 3, 1914; he assured him that, if war broke out, he would still allow Germans to do their business in Hong Kong under oath that they would not seek to damage British interests. Britain declared war on August 5. That day, May wrote a letter by hand to the consul, "My dear Voretzsch, I am grieved to tell you that the worst has happened and that our countries are now at war. I would give my life if I could avert such a catastrophe by so doing." Becker said that relations between the Germans and the British in Hong Kong were "relaxed, friendly and good".

Britain's declaration of war against Germany on August 4 changed everything. A few days later, the Hong Kong government put enemy aliens, including Germans, under parole; they were restricted to certain areas and had to report to the police at stated times. On August 12, May was ordered by his superiors in London to close down the German consulate; this left the consulate of the US, a neutral nation, responsible for German and Austrian civilians. The citizens of 'enemy countries' were still allowed to continue doing business. In the last week of October, Germany issued a call-up of its military and naval reserves. The Hong Kong government issued an order to intern German men of military age. On October 30, German companies wrote a joint letter to the government, sent through the US consulate, arguing that, considering their great contribution to the economy of Hong Kong, they should be able to go on working. It said that while they were naturally trading for their own benefit, they thought that they might justly claim to have contributed in no small way to the development and growth of prosperity of the Colony. In their capacity as peaceful traders, they considered themselves and their businesses a valuable asset to the community "It has taken decades of hard work to create such an asset, which they consider particularly valuable to the Colony since they have as impartial traders been instrumental to a great extent in attracting to this part business from all quarters of the globe, thereby promoting British trade more than that of any other nation." It was signed by thirty-four companies, of whom ten were in the process of being liquidated. They listed the years of their foundation in Hong Kong, with the earliest, Siemssen & Co, dating back to 1848.

But, after the outbreak of fighting in Europe, there was no space for compromise. From October 1914, German businesses were confiscated and about 200 German men of military age interned, first in Stonecutters Island and later at a camp in Hung Hom. They were guarded by members of the Hong Kong Volunteer Force. They were put to work sweeping the streets and performing other manual tasks. Two years later, the internees were sent to an internment camp in Holsworthy near Liverpool, New South Wales in Australia. Those above military age, wives and children were deported to Shanghai and Manila. Among the properties confiscated by the government was the imposing

German Club on 7 Kennedy Road. In September 1918, it was handed over to St Joseph's College, a Catholic secondary school. The Germans who were interned were not released until after the war. They were deported to Germany and their properties were not returned. In 1921, there were only three Germans left in Hong Kong.

Among the German firms liquidated was Arnold & Co, which had been founded in 1866 as a small trading company in Shameen Island, Guangzhou, by Jacob Arnhold, a German Jewish businessman, and Peter Karberg, a Danish merchant. In 1867, they opened an office in Hong Kong and in 1881 established their headquarters in Shanghai; it was the beginning of a strong business presence in Hong Kong and throughout China. By the turn of the century, the firm had thirty-seven offices, with buying offices in London, Manchester, Berlin and New York. In 1914, it was controlled by Harry and Charles Arnold, both of whom had British nationality. But the government was suspicious of the firm's German sympathies. Its head man in Hong Kong, a German national, had to resign his seat on the board of HSBC and was interned. In the 1930s, the Sassoon Group obtained a controlling interest in Arnhold. Its business flourished until 1949 when, with the change of government in China, the headquarters relocated to Hong Kong. Maurice Green, who had been associated with the company since the Sassoon takeover, acquired the controlling interest in Arnhold in 1957. Today, according to its website, Arnhold Group is a leading distributor of building materials in Hong Kong and China. Headquartered in Hong Kong, Arnhold also has sales offices in Macau and in Shanghai, and a stone-processing factory in Guangdong Province. Sales of the Arnhold Group are derived from two main business areas—building materials and engineering equipment. The group serves an extensive network of customers, including property developers, contractors, utility companies and government departments. These draconian measures did not apply to French, Belgian and citizens of countries allied to Britain during World War I; their companies here were not affected.

Recovery
During World War I, the colonial government shut down German businesses and interned their German staff. After the war, the firms received no compensation for their losses. Some returned to Hong Kong. Arnold, Karberg & Co changed its name to Arnhold & Co and became British; the company continues today, under new ownership. Hesse, Ehlers & Co opened in Hong Kong in July 1861. After World War I, it reopened in the city, dealing mainly in machinery. Melchers & Co opened in Hong Kong in 1866. After liquidation here during World War I, it reopened in 1922 in Hong Kong and Shanghai, and later in other cities. It went through the same experience in World War II; then it reopened in 1952 and is thriving today. In 2016, it celebrated its 150 years in Asia and China.

BASF, the world's largest chemical company, has a connection of more than 120 years with Hong Kong. Today it is one of the biggest foreign investors in China and is spending US$10 billion on a giant new production site in Zhanjiang, Guangdong Province. It has been selling goods to China for more than 120 years – and Hong Kong has played a key role in facilitating these sales.

Friedrich Engelhorn founded Badische Anilin & Soda-Fabrik (Baden Aniline and Soda Factory) in Mannheim, Germany on April 6, 1865. It was in November 1885 that the company decided to send a deputy director to China and Japan, as a first step to exporting to these countries. In the 1880s, it began to sell textile dyes in Greater China. In 1897, it signed a contract with Jebsen

& Co, a trading company founded in Hong Kong in 1895 by two German cousins; it would represent BASF in southern China, from Fujian to Yunnan Provinces. The German company had a separate agent to represent it in Shanghai and Northern China. This partnership with Jebsen lasted until the end of 1981, a co-operation of eighty-five years with four generations of the Jebsen family. Due to the new arrangement, BASF sales in southern China grew rapidly, from US$46,000 in 1897 to US$479,000 in 1910 and US$832,000 in 1913. The main products were dyes and auxiliary agents used to color wool, silk and cotton. Between 1890 and 1916, BASF sales in Germany grew by more ninety percent and those in China rise eight-fold. BASF and Jebsen together built a dye work in Foshan, Guangdong Province, where they took Chinese customers to see for themselves the speed and efficiency of the production processes. By 1913, BASF sales to China accounted for fourteen percent of its total turnover of nearly 120 million marks, up from 5.6 percent of about 51 million Deutschmarks in 1904. Jebsen played a key role in this growth, with its knowledge of and connections with the local market.

After the start of World War I in August 1914, the ships of the Jebsen company in Hong Kong were confiscated and its businesses wound up. Jacob Jensen was interned, together with the other German citizens. BASF's large stock of indigo was taken over by Chao Yue-teng (趙月騰), the comprador of Jebsen & Co since 1896. The price of this indigo increased greatly; Chao sold it, providing the fortune that allowed him to launch his own company. After the end of the war, he gave Jebsen & Co US$40,000 in starting capital, urgently needed to restart the dyeing business of BASF. After its defeat, Germany was forced to share many important patents for its processes with the victorious powers. BASF faced stiffer competition from rival firms, from Britain, Japan and the United States. It began to sell chemical fertilizer

EUROPEANS IN HONG KONG

to China.

To regain the markets lost after World War I, BASF joined with five other German chemical firms to form a new company called I.G. Farben, which became the largest chemical corporation in the world. It decided to lay off its foreign representatives and open its own sales offices; for this purpose, Defag, the German dye corporation, was founded in China on January 1, 1927. Its Hong Kong partner, Jebsen & Co, was given the Defag suboffice in Guangzhou, the sales organization for indigo it had established and representation of the nitrogen business throughout southern China. In the middle of 1925, Jebsen had moved its headquarters from Guangzhou to Hong Kong to serve customers faster. During World War II, Jebsen continued its operations in China. In 1946, after the defeat of Nazi Germany, all the assets of I.G. Farben in China were confiscated as enemy property and the German employees had to leave, to return to their war-ravaged homeland or another country. In November 1945, in West Germany, the Allied Control Council of the victorious power ordered the dissolution of I.G. Farben. From 1947 to 1948, the U.S. authorities tried 23 IG Farben directors for war crimes, and 13 were convicted. During World War Two, they used slave labour from concentration camps; one subsidiary produced the poison gas Zyklon B, which killed over one million people in gas chambers during the Holocaust. In 1952, BASF was reestablished as one of the successor companies of the dissolved firm. In November 1947, Michael Jebsen, sole owner of Jebsen & Co since 1944, visited the BASF headquarters in Ludwigshafen and asked to be its representative in China again. He fought off the competition and was chosen for this role in November 1950, as sole representative. Business with the People's Republic of China became difficult, especially after the new government established diplomatic relations with East Germany on October

27, 1949; the two countries signed a friendship treaty. From 1955 to 1969, the government of West Germany practised the Hallstein Doctrine, named after Walter Hallstein, Secretary of State in the Foreign Office. This stated that West Germany would consider any new diplomatic relations between a country and East Germany as an unfriendly act. In February 1957, Hallstein visited the Jebsen & Co headquarters in Hong Kong. They asked him how China could improve relations with his government; he replied that it would have to recognize West Germany. Jebsen & Co had to do business through the Guangzhou Trade Fair, held twice a year, one of the few opportunities to negotiate agreements with representatives of state foreign trade firms. Since China had only a limited amount of foreign currency, these deals were often in the form of barter. Jebsen's wide connections with German companies enabled him to reach such deals. In the Spring Fair of 1975, for example, it sold Bosch auto parts, Merck vitamins, Schering hormones, copper pipes, crankshafts, Siemens chart recorders and, for the first time, 7,000 metric tonnes of urea from BASF with a total value of 6.2 million Deutschmarks. In exchange, it acquired Chinese goat skins, honey, real hair for wigs, tobacco, eucalyptus oil, peanuts and walnuts worth 5.6 million Deutschmarks, to sell into western markets.

In October 1972, West Germany and the People's Republic of China established diplomatic relations. This made trade between the two sides much easier. That year BASF signed a new agreement with Jebsen. The German company's revenue had reached a record twelve billion Deutschmarks. Jebsen sold its products to about thirty different industries in China. But the nature of the business was changing. BASF wanted to build production facilities in China, which Beijing welcomed. The negotiations were long and tortuous. BASF opened its own company in Hong Kong, with the name BASF Far East Ltd in 1976 and renamed as BASF China Ltd in 1982. This was the first step toward building its own large-scale organization in China and parting ways with Jebsen. In April 1981, the company's Board of Executive Directors decided to end their co-operation with the Hong Kong firm Jebsen & Co. The divorce of this eighty-five-year-old marriage was amicable.

In 1995, BASF established its East Asia Regional Headquarters in Hong Kong, with a member of the Board of Executive Directors being located in the Asia Pacific for the first time. Since then, BASF's headquarters for the Asia Pacific region, where the company employs more than 18,600 employees at about 100 sites, has remained in Hong Kong, where it employs more than 450 people. Jebsen & Co played an important role in BASF's success in China.

Third Generation of Family Business
For Jebsen & Co, BASF was one of its most important customers. After more than 120 years in Hong Kong, it remains today a family company and is headed by Hans Michael Jebsen. Here is his profile:

Hans Michael Jebsen (捷成漢) is the third generation of his family to lead the company founded by his grandfather Jacob Jebsen and Heinrich Jessen in March 1895. In 2020, Jebsen & Co celebrated its 125th year; it employs 2,100 people in Greater China and operates in fifteen countries. In 2018, it had an annual turnover of HK$14.8 billion. It remains family-owned and headquartered in Hong Kong. Jebsen lives with his German wife Desiree and their five children on the Peak.

He was born on November 15, 1956, in Siegen, Germany, into a family of German-Danish origin. He was the son of Hans Jacob Jensen; his uncle Michael Jebsen served as chairman of the company and died on May 1, 2000, aged eighty-eight. Hans

Michael attended the Deutsches Gymnasium in Aabenraa, the family's hometown in southern Denmark. After graduating in 1975, he completed a two-year banking traineeship in Flensburg and Hamburg and spent almost two years in London interning for the merchant bank, Gray Dawes & Co and private bank Anthony Gibbs & Sons. Then he went to the University of St Gallen, Switzerland, to study economics and business management. During the holidays, his father took him to Hong Kong, so that he could become familiar with the city. In 1981, he moved to Hong Kong as a minted partner and director; he was just twenty-four. Before taking up his new post, he spent several months in China, including at the company's newly revived Beijing liaison office. He explored the countryside around the city. The task of fitting into the company hierarchy was not an easy one for an incoming young man. Michael Jebsen was an autocrat, used to being in sole charge.

Through his business and community life, Hans Michael has built up a global network of contacts. In addition, he is on the boards of Hysan Development Co Ltd and Wharf (Holdings) Ltd in Hong Kong, as well as Danfoss A/S, Denmark. He was awarded the Bronze Bauhinia Star of the Hong Kong SAR in 2001 and has been an honorary citizen of Jilin City since 2005. In 2006, he was awarded the Silver Cross of the Order of the Dannebrog by order of H.M. the Queen of Denmark. In 2008, he was also awarded the Cross of the Order of Merit of the Federal Republic of Germany. In 2014, he was made Knight 1st Class of the Order of the Dannebrog.

In 1995, to mark the 100th anniversary of the firm, the partners launched the Jebsen Education Fund, with HK$20 million, to provide educational opportunities for people in Hong Kong and China. Jebsen & Co Ltd had long placed a premium on education and training; Hans Michael Jebsen himself has helped put the children of several employees through university over the years. He is active in charities and NGOs. He is chairman of the Asian Cultural Council Hong Kong Friends' Committee, a trustee of the World Wide Fund for Nature in Hong Kong, and a member of the Advisory Board of the Hong Kong Red Cross. He is also chairman of the Asian Cultural Council in Hong Kong and vice-chairman of the Asian Cultural Council of New York. In Denmark, he owns many historic properties, as well as historic inns and hotels. In 2015, the Hong Kong University of Science and Technology awarded him a Doctor of Business Administration honoris causa. He is married to Désirée Jebsen, a former countess of Schaffgotsch.

In an interview, Jebsen said that he grew up in the knowledge that his father wished him to take on the family business. Their home had Chinese artifacts and the family had Chinese friends. In 1981, at the age of 24, he became a director of the company in Hong Kong, because of the premature death of his father in 1979. "I was catapulted into a business environment at a young age. I was aware that my role was to learn, listen and adapt fast. Various mentors were extremely helpful, including my uncle and Chairman of the company and senior members of the company management, both European and Chinese. I soon swam like fish in water."

The dramatic changes caused by the reform and open-door policy disrupted the firm's traditional entrepôt trader business model. It had to find a new niche. "This is easier said than done. Naturally we went through trials and errors, with initially 'too many irons in the fire' at the same time. Yet, this is entrepreneurism: learning by doing including mistakes. Our company had to reinvent itself more than once during the past. From being a shipping and trading company as 'general or sole agents', we became a company providing products and services in a number of defined areas, such as chemical, technical, consumer, etc. Today, we are even more focused in the areas of motors distribution, beverage, consumer and automation businesses." The firm has also made selected investments as both majority and minority partners in various fast and often innovative developing business sectors, in China and beyond.

In 1971, his father refused an offer from Jardine Matheson to take over the firm. He has continued this policy. "Retaining our independence, however, is paramount, so we never felt the temptation to go for a listing on the stock exchange or sell our business. But we are open to partnerships in our various business lines, which we have successfully demonstrated. This very much remains our philosophy today." He said the company has enjoyed a particularly high loyalty among staff because it has created an environment in which individuals could thrive without feeling as if they were in a straitjacket. "With Mainland China being our most dynamic market, it is paramount that we instill a dynamic corporate culture in all our activities. Also, importantly, we must remain an attractive employer of talent," he said. He and his wife have been active in arts, culture, education and the community at large, as well as CSR programs in the company. His wife has taken a particular interest in education and helping people in need. As a father, he hopes that the business will remain in the family. "To make a successful entrepreneur takes a lot of dedication, passion and commitment and at times sacrifice. This can never be delivered credibly out of the sense of loyalty to fulfill parents' expectations. Our eldest son has shown interest from an early age and has earmarked his education and career for a future role in the company, hopefully one day as my successor," he said.

After World War II, Dieter David von Hansemann was in 1951 the first German national to be allowed to settle in Hong Kong; he worked for Jebsen & Co He was the pioneer of a

EUROPEANS IN HONG KONG

German business community that grew rapidly after the war, to take advantage of the city's many opportunities. The German government moved quickly to restore relations with Hong Kong. It opened its consulate general on July 27, 1953. One of the first businessman to come was Hans Dieter Isler, who arrived in 1954 to open the office of a Hamburg trading company. In 1958, Deutsche Bank established an office in the city. Its operations here now are one of the bank's hubs in the Asia Pacific region. It first arrived here in 1900, as a branch of Deutsch-Asiatische Bank that was closed during World War I. In 1986, it acquired European Asian Bank, including its operations in Hong Kong. In 1961, Lufthansa landed for the first time at Kai Tak airport, with a Boeing 707 which had come via Rome, Cairo, Karachi, Calcutta and Bangkok.

In 1979, Commerzbank opened its Hong Kong branch. On October 5, 1982, the German Business Association (GBA) was registered with 128 members. By 1991, its membership had grown to 375; in 1999, it became the German Chamber of Commerce. In May 2019, GCC and German Industry and Commerce (GIC) — a member of the German Chambers of Commerce Abroad (Auslandshandelskammern) — moved into new premises in Causeway Bay, after being based in Admiralty since 1996. Today the Chamber has more than 400 members.

Since 2009, Hong Kong has had its own mission in Berlin, the Hong Kong Economic and Trade Office (HKETO). The Hong Kong Trade Development Council (HKTDC) has a regional office for Europe based in Frankfurt. In February 1998, Germany and Hong Kong signed an agreement for the Encouragement and Reciprocal Protection of Investments. During 2019, 217,779 Germans visited Hong Kong.

Major German firms in Hong Kong include BASF, Bayer, law firm CMS Hasche Sigle, Deutsche Post DHL, Hapag Lloyd,

Henkel AG, software company SAP, Siemens and Volkswagen, Financial institutions include Deutsche Bank, DZ Bank and Commerzbank AG and Allianz Insurance.

In the 1980s, with the beginning of China's open-door policy, more and more Germans started to set up their own companies in the city. Until then, many firms had been represented by famous trading houses like Jebsen, Melchers, Illies, Rieckermann and others; they counted many of the big German corporates among their principals. In the 1980s, companies like Siemens, Lufthansa, BASF and famous car brands started their own presence in Hong Kong to seize the opportunities in China. At that time, setting up across the border was still a major undertaking; for most smaller businesses, it was too cumbersome and expensive. Hong Kong offered a relatively cheap and efficient alternative and the enormous convenience of having all the China expertise one needed, concentrated in one easily accessible spot. Back then, Hong Kong was more or less the sole gateway to and from China.

Today the Germans are one of the most important members of the European community in Hong Kong, numbering 4,000 residents. There are approximately 600 German companies based here, half of which use Hong Kong as the home base for the Asia-Pacific region. For them, it is a base for doing business with not only the Mainland but also Japan, Korea, Southeast Asia, India, Australia and New Zealand. Most of the German residents are business people and their families. For the last sixty years, the city has provided them with an excellent base to do business and a comfortable place for their families to reside, go to school and enjoy the lifestyle they wish.

Germany is Hong Kong's largest trading partner in the European Union and ranks eleventh among Hong Kong's trading partners in the world. In 2019, bilateral trade amounted to €13.97 billion. Hong Kong also plays a significant role in the trade

EUROPEANS IN HONG KONG

between the Mainland and Germany, with about 5.6 per cent of the trade routed through Hong Kong in 2019; this amounted to €9.84 billion euros. In 2019, Hong Kong's main exports to Germany were jewelry, printed matter, semi-conductors and electronic valves and tubes. Hong Kong's main imports from Germany were automobiles, machinery, electrical and electronic goods, luxury goods and foodstuffs. German brands account for 75 percent of all premium cars in Hong Kong.

Three Profiles
Next are profiles of three German businessmen who have spent most of their professional lives in Hong Kong. Two of them live here today, and the third stayed for thirty-two years before retiring in Indonesia. Each ran their own company and were pioneers in the China market after it opened the door to foreign trade and investment in 1980. Hong Kong and China have given them the opportunity to take part in the economic miracle of China and earn an excellent living out of it.

Till Freyer, a German, lived in Hong Kong from 1959 until 1991 and worked in the garment industry. He earned the title of 'The King of Shirts' because of a single order of 1.2 million shirts worth nearly US$3 million, believed to be the biggest of its kind in Hong Kong in the 1960s. His successful career was possible because Chinese factory owners here needed foreigners like him to market their garments to buyers in Europe and North America. Since then, the internet, instant communication, rapid transcontinental travel and a dramatic increase in western-educated Asians have made such a person a less valuable commodity.

Freyer, who lives today in retirement in Bogor, Indonesia, describes his eventful life in his autobiography, *The King of Shirts*, published in 2014. Born in 1935, he graduated from high school and went to work for a well-established export company in Hamburg in 1958. The next year, it sent him with six travel cases full of samples on a sales mission through the Middle East, ending in Singapore. Instead of returning to Hamburg and collecting his substantial commission, however, he spent his final dollars on a Cathay Pacific flight to Hong Kong

He was fortunate to find a job quickly with a British trading company W.R. Loxley & Co. It hired him to develop an export business for consumer goods, including apparel. He started work in July 1959. His timing was excellent. Hundreds of manufacturers had moved their operations from the Mainland to Hong Kong and resumed production. They needed customers in the richest countries — in North America and Western Europe.

"The first factories to export garments to Europe and Asia were located in Japan," he wrote. "Production cost increases in Japan resulted in the move of such operations to Hong Kong. The British colony enjoyed a duty-free status except for very few luxury items and had an eager employment-seeking workforce, ideal for a garment industry. Luck was on my side to have arrived in Hong Kong when the business was being transferred from Japan to Hong Kong ... From 1959 to 1969, industrial entrepreneurs in Hong Kong were exclusively Chinese, mainly from Shanghai. They did an excellent job setting up and running production facilities but knew very little, if anything, about export marketing, merchandizing and customers. This allowed international companies like Loxley and others to become an essential link and a welcome business partner for factories in Hong Kong."

What Freyer and other expatriates provided were foreign languages, knowledge of and personal connections with overseas markets and the ease of operating in them. At the same time, most European and American companies did not want the trouble and expense of setting up an office in Asia; in the early 1960s, a flight from Frankfurt to Hong Kong took thirty-two hours, with four or five stopovers. It was easier to hire firms like Loxley to work on their behalf. Germany became its most important market and garments the best-selling product line.

"Hong Kong became the world's unchallenged 'Sewing Center of the World'. Garments represented well over fifty percent of all exports, which only started to decline in the last 1980s," Freyer said. "Textiles and apparel became the main engine of the HK economy and accounted for nearly 500,000 jobs in nearly 18,000 factories at their peak. By 1980, sales value reached HK$45 billion."

Freyer's biggest deal came from the Soviet government, which wanted shirts for people in Bulgaria—this won him the title 'King of Shirts. The order was 1.2 million pieces of men's Nyltest Dress Shirts, one style and white. They were to be made of warp-knitted nylon fabric and needed no ironing. "The fabric was most uncomfortable to wear. It made the wearer feel like being in a sauna and was a short-term success only. It was very cheap, US$0.48 per meter in 36 inches width." The value of the order was US$2.976 million FOB (free on board). The Russians placed the order with a company in Finland, which passed it to a garment factory in Sweden; it did not have the production capacity and asked a German trading company that gave the work to Freyer. He placed the order with three factories in Hong Kong and two in South Korea. The Russians were told that the production was being done in Sweden; the deliveries were made via Sweden. Loxley made a gross margin of 5.2 percent, a gross income of US$154,752, "excellent for such a quantity. This was the most rewarding order which I have ever handled, a triumph of trade, finance, diplomacy, cooperation: my best ever transaction. Such business is no longer possible today. Global trading, access to worldwide supply sources via the internet and open markets have made it increasingly difficult to guard business secrets."

In December 1964, he left Loxley to work in a new company in which a German firm held a fifty per cent share and he and Loxley twenty-five per cent each. He worked there for eight years before setting up his own company. He enjoyed the expatriate life, with membership of the Hong Kong Country Club and purchase of a Chinese junk, custom-built by a small boatyard in Aberdeen. He named it 'Schnaps' and moored it in Hebe Haven, with beautiful beaches and crystal-clear water. He spent many nights on the boat with his wife and four children.

The garment business is exhausting. Competition is intense; styles and fashion change all the time. Over fifty-five years, Freyer made more than 500 voyages between Asia and Europe. As production costs in Hong Kong rose, so the industry migrated to the Mainland, Vietnam, Thailand and other countries. Freyer had to visit these countries to inspect possible production sites. The business became more complicated in 1974 with the imposition of export quotas imposed by the importing countries. "They lasted for about thirty years before such useless restrictions were lifted. They did not protect a single factory in a garment-importing country, it only added to the cost price which consumers had to pay." Manufacturers shifted production to countries not subject to quota, including Laos, Cambodia, Bangladesh and Pakistan. They also used 'submarine business", under which goods were produced in Hong Kong or the Mainland, but the Certificate of Origin was obtained from a third, quota-free country. The biggest supplier of such documents was Indonesia. "It was a great relief and a giant step toward global trading when quota restrictions were lifted about thirty years after having been introduced," he said. In August 1991, Freyer moved to Bogor in Indonesia and retired from business at the end of 2000.

EUROPEANS IN HONG KONG

Jurgen Kracht arrived in Hong Kong from Germany in 1971 to work in a trading company. In 1982, he and his wife set up a management consulting firm, which in 2022 celebrated its fortieth year, with son Stephan as managing director. With headquarters in Hong Kong, it has five offices and a staff of 130. Most of its clients are from Germany, Austria and Switzerland. During his lifetime, Kracht has witnessed—and helped to create—the remarkable success of German companies in China, where they are the biggest investor and trading partner from Europe.

Kracht was born in 1950 in Lemgo, a small town halfway between Hanover and Dusseldorf in the north of Germany. He studied International Business Studies at the University of Bremen. On graduation, in the summer of 1970, he and a college friend took a trip to Japan. This included a stop in Hong Kong; he was impressed by its speed and dynamism and sense of safety. In Siberia, the two had a first-hand look at Soviet communism—heavy drinking of vodka and the refusal of their guide to show them Christian churches or Jewish synagogues, because they were not on the official tour route. The two returned to Europe via the trans-Siberian railway from Vladivostok; they ran out of money in Helsinki, Finland, and had to ask their parents for help. Back home, Kracht read sixty pages of job advertisements in the *Frankfurt Allgemeine Zeitung* newspaper and applied for one at Jebsen & Co, a Danish-German trading company in Hong Kong. Three days later, he went to Hamburg for an interview and was accepted. His job was to sell chemicals made by BASF, one of Jebsen's biggest clients. He was sent for four months' training at BASF headquarters at Ludwigshafen, to learn about its products.

He arrived in Hong Kong on January 5, 1971. No one was at Kai Tak airport to greet him. Jebsen & Co was a major trading company, with a staff of 1,500 and 400 company clients, mainly from the German-speaking world. He was one of thirty bachelors from Germany and Denmark working in the firm. He lived with two of them in a flat in United Mansion in Shui Fai Terrace in Wanchai; they had a Shanghainese maid and cook, husband and wife, who made them three meals a day. Each bachelor had his own bedroom and bathroom. The company provided him with a Volkswagen Beetle car, radio, television, camera and record player; he paid for them in instalments taken out of his salary. "It was a fantastic time. We spent a lot of time in bars. One day we drove the Beetle down a narrow street in Wanchai. A colleague stopped it and opened the front. "I lost my engine," he declared to an astonished crowd (in a Beetle, the engine is in the rear of the car). So Chinese people helped us to push the car." In 1972, he married Cynthia, who was working in a German company in Hong Kong. One of his duties was to attend the Canton Trade Fair twice a year; it was the only opportunity to conduct business with Chinese trade corporations. The years with Jebsen were an invaluable education in the Chinese market.

After eleven years in Hong Kong, on the advice of a friend, Kracht and his wife decided to set up their own consulting company. Fiducia Management Consultants (FMC, 德信管理咨詢) was born on June 18, 1982, with registered capital of HK$100,000, in a rented apartment in Elizabeth House in Causeway Bay. "My colleagues laughed at me," he said. "They said that no one would pay for consultancy. Everyone else was in trading. Hong Kong had thousands of trading companies." He found his first clients by going to the offices of the Hong Kong Trade Development Council in Hamburg, Vienna, Frankfurt and Zurich and seeking companies that wanted to sell or buy from China and had no presence in the Far East. "The clients did not pay for consulting but for solutions. A Hamburg company was supplying jute bags to the government of Saudi Arabia. It

EUROPEANS IN HONG KONG

gave them to farmers full of barley to feed to their animals. The company wanted jute bags." Kracht found a company in Sichuan able to produce large volumes of high-quality bags. He gave them three printers and ink, so that they could print the name of the Saudi government in Arabic on the bags. Fiducia had to provide what its clients need—searching for customers and suppliers and negotiation support. When a German company wanted a manager for its China operations, they found one. When a firm needed bookkeeping, they hired an accountant. Kracht accompanied clients on business trips to China, to meet clients and negotiate deals. He knew better than they the tricks and stratagems of the Chinese side. He helped clients find a site in China and set up manufacturing operations there; the services included selecting a factory manager and staff, doing the necessary background checks and negotiating with the local government. Fiducia gradually broadened its expertise—advice in setting up a corporate operation, market research, tax and accounting, executive search and Enterprise Resource Planning (ERP) software solutions. Its website says: "we have a vast network of industry specialists, associations, university bodies, government agencies and legal advisers, and long-standing expertise in sectors, including automotive, chemicals and plastics, consumer goods, electronics, fashion and textiles, machinery, medical technology and private equity."

Fiducia's client portfolio included Chinese companies that wanted to export to Europe. It helped them find customers, especially at European trade fairs. The Chinese firms quickly learned about market expectations with respect to quality and design. Many have become global leaders in their sectors and no longer require the help of middlemen like Fiducia.

Today the firm has offices in Hong Kong, Shenzhen, Shanghai, Beijing and Munich, with a staff of 130, of whom seventy-eighty are in the Mainland. Jurgen and Cynthia have one son and two daughters. They were always hoping that their son Stephan (葛一凡) would take over the firm, so that it would remain a family business. Stephan spent the first fifteen years of his life in Hong Kong; he received his primary and secondary education there. When he was fifteen, his parents sent him to St Blasein College, a Jesuit boarding school in the Black Forest in southern Germany, close to the border with Switzerland. "It was the best decision of our life. It is an excellent school, for study and moral values. It was the first school in Germany to accept Chinese children and to teach Mandarin," Kracht said. From there, Stephan went to study Economics at the London School of Economics and Political Science; on graduation, he worked with Bain & Company, a global management consultancy. Then he spent four years in Shanghai, where he opened his own trading company with a friend. "It was very good entrepreneur training for him. The competition was cut-throat. We never talked to him about taking over Fiducia. We left it entirely up to him." Cynthia said that her greatest experience came at 2030 on November 11, 2004, in Shanghai where their son Stephan announced that he was ready to join the family business. "We were assured of continuity in Fiducia," she said. He took over as managing director in 2012. Jurgen said that today he worked three days a week in the company, on strategy and special projects, and his wife not at all. "Stephan runs the business from day to day. There can only be one managing director. On major decisions, he will consult me. One challenge we face is the different mindset between our staff in Hong Kong and in the Mainland. A majority are in the Mainland. They believe that Hong Kong has been well treated and should not complain." Outside companies, including banks, have made offers to buy Fiducia. "We considered them but declined. If you sell out, what do you do with yourself? Those with wealth lose their grounding."

Kracht is a member of the Hong Kong Club, the Foreign Correspondents' Club and the Royal Hong Kong Yacht Club. He has been an honorary adviser to the Management Consultancies Association of Hong Kong since 2015. He and his wife live in an apartment of 2,000 square feet in Parkview (陽明山莊) at the top of Repulse Bay Road; from one window, they can see Aberdeen and, from another, Wanchai. They bought it in 2010 for HK$20 million. At seventy, he retains his enthusiasm for China, collecting information and stories like a journalist. He contributes articles to newspapers and magazines and is a popular speaker at China events.

Through his company, Kracht has witnessed from the front line one of the most remarkable transformations in history — how China has changed from an inward-looking country reliant on agriculture into the world's second-largest economy. Of the countries in Europe, none has benefited more from this transformation than Germany. Its companies have invested more than any other EU country, especially in the automotive sector. Its products are market leaders in China, in automobiles, machinery, chemicals, medical equipment, cosmetics and other fields. More than 5,000 German companies operate there. China is easily Germany's biggest trade partner, with the trade volume reaching €206 billion euros (US$233 billion) in 2019. The EU as a whole is China's second-largest trade partner, after the United States.

So Fiducia has been a company in the right place at the right time. Its niche in the fiercely competitive market for professional services has been companies from German-speaking companies — the biggest European investors in and traders with China. Why have German companies been so successful?

"German multinationals were smart in staffing: rather than

sending people from Germany directly, the company posted executives who worked in places like Moscow or Jakarta—they knew how to operate in challenging markets. The success of German firms is due to their approach, patient attitude, and the willingness to wait for results. German politicians were supportive of these pioneers too. For example, former Chancellor Helmut Schmidt visited China every year and formed very good relations with paramount leader Deng Xiaoping and former President Jiang Zemin. Chancellor Angela Merkel went there twelve times, more than any other Western leader.

"German firms are viewed as a reliable business partner because of their actions. Their word is their word, a handshake is a handshake. Chinese know that German goods are more expensive but they recognize that they are of high quality and reliable. That image is strongly embedded in China. One of the chief reasons for Germany's success in China is the strength of its manufacturing. A big part of that comes down to the country's Mittelstand—the thousands of small- and medium-sized industrial firms that are the heart of the German economy. There is a growing awareness in Beijing that the backbone of a healthy industry is not the massive companies but the family companies like those of the Mittelstand. In fact, the Chinese government views the German economic structure as a model. I understand that the Economics Department of the Chinese Embassy in Berlin mirrors the structure of the German manufacturing industry. Their task is to observe and understand how German companies tick, particularly the Mittelstand. A big part of our business is advising those Mittelstand manufacturing companies. They are not shy about going to China, but value our support and advice. So there's been a big expansion in Mittelstand firms entering China? Yes, the big expansion of companies opening Chinese factories was between 2000 and 2010 after China permitted subsidiary companies besides joint ventures. As an example, the city of Taicang in Jiangsu Province today houses 120 German companies, mostly from the Stuttgart area. They are all Mittelstand manufacturing firms and they all know each other from home. The companies agreed not to poach each other's staff; also they have set up an apprentice scheme just like back home."

Hans Joachim Isler was born in Hong Kong in 1968 and has lived there ever since, except for eight years of education in Germany. He has taken over the trading firm which his father founded in 1962. "I am always happy to be in Germany, but I feel more at home here. I plan to stay and do not consider retirement. I am very attached to Hong Kong." A fervent sailor, Isler is a member of the Harborfront Commission.

Father Hans Dieter Isler arrived in Hong Kong in 1954, to open the office of a Hamburg trading company; he joined a very small German community. There was hostility lingering after World War II. He had an office next to the Hong Kong Club but was advised not to apply.

Born in 1929, Father was undergoing military training in 1945 when the war in Europe ended; he was fortunate the war ended before he was compelled to take part in any fighting. He was living in Bremen, one of the cities most heavily damaged by Allied bombing. After graduating from high school, he served an apprenticeship at the German Cotton Trade Council, where he learned the textile business. Then he joined a trading firm in Hamburg after setting the condition that, after two years, they send him overseas; they accepted this condition. Hans said: "He was living in a hungry, destroyed Germany. He wanted to go abroad."

The firm offered him Hong Kong and Apia, Western Samoa, where it had a well-established office. "He chose Hong Kong because it would be a new office and he could do things his way. He was very brave. Friends advised him not to go, saying that it was a dull, sleepy city." For the first eight years, he worked for the original trading firm, building up the business. Then, in 1962, he decided to set up his own firm, HD Isler & Co.

Hans said: "He used all his savings, with no outside capital. By then, he knew the business and had contacts with suppliers and customers. He saw a big opportunity in the textile business, with the arrival of jet planes, telex and the new connectivity, and forecast a rapid increase in trade. He was proved exactly right." The firm imported items like chemicals and construction materials from Germany.

He married a woman introduced by a mutual friend. Hans Joachim was born in 1968. Like his four siblings, he was educated at the German Swiss International School here. "My father was one of the key drivers of the school. It was imperative for the growing presence of German families in Hong Kong." At sixteen, Hans Joachim went to spend four years at the Kolleg St Blasien, a Jesuit male boarding school in the Black Forest in southern Germany. "It was a complete change. I learned independence. The Jesuits are good educators and proponents of science and study. They know how to get results. They were strict and helped me cultivate an interest in sports and study. We had a strong camaraderie among the students. Friends I made then I still have today." He then studied Business Management, Economy and Trade at a university outside Wiesbaden, followed by one year working at a clothing firm in Munich.

In 1989, the Berlin Wall fell. In 1991, the Soviet Union collapsed and Europe had been reunified. "I was very comfortable living in Germany. I had friends living in different cities and knew it well.

EUROPEANS IN HONG KONG

It was not a given that I had to come back to the family firm. My father said that I must be educated and do well. It was not an open door for me. Many friends said that Europe was the future. I said that China was also the future, with Hong Kong playing a pivotal role. My father wanted to see the firm remain in the family and was keen to see me return. My two sisters both worked in the firm before they married and went to Europe. One brother is also in Europe; my youngest brother works in the firm." In 1993, he returned from Germany and started in the firm. In 1995, he became managing director, when his father stepped down to become chairman, a position he held until 2020. "He approved strategic decisions, and investments."

As a small trading company in a highly competitive field, HD Isler had to make its niche in the market. "Others can always offer a cheaper price. So we compete on a service which others cannot provide, on quality, development and design," Isler said. "Most of our clients are in Germany. We know the market there well, especially the medium to high-end. People are familiar with our name. We know the requirements of the market. Germans are conservative." He goes to Germany eight to ten times a year, to see customers and the market. "This is a physical business, you need to feel the product and the fabric. You must see the clients. In our business, things change quickly. You must help customers with these changes." He has a similar approach with the companies that make their garments. Initially, the factories were all in Hong Kong, then southeast China and now mainly in the Yangtze River area—Nanjing, Ningbo and Hangzhou, as well as in Qingdao and Dalian. "I am very hands-on. I like to see suppliers and the production myself." So, before the pandemic, he visited China every six weeks for this purpose. He also visits Taiwan, South Korea and Japan to meet the companies that supply the raw materials for the company's garments. In 2017, he served as the President of the German Chamber of Commerce in Hong Kong.

Over the last ten years, the business environment has changed for the worse.

"The major companies, like H&M, Zara and Uniqlo, have set up their own buying offices and deal directly with producers. They have huge volume and their own retail networks. They turn out new designs every year. This has turned the lower end of the market upside down. The consumer has benefited in terms of fashionable clothes at lower prices." At the other end of the market are luxury brands like Dior, Prada and Montclair, which sell clothes at high prices; they are a status symbol as well as being of excellent quality. "We are in the middle market, with brands at reasonable prices. This is our key market and it is melting away. In addition, the spending habits of young people are changing — less on fashion and more on holidays, going out, electronics and lifestyle. There are many people and brands in the garment business and there is oversupply." HD Isler is supplying smaller companies that do not have offices in the Far East and sells items other than garments, such as protective clothing. Asked if he would like his son to take over the firm, he said that the young boy was only seven. "Perhaps he will join professions that do not exist now. Perhaps our firm will sell other products."

Outside work, his passion is sailing and watersports. He was a board member of the Royal Hong Kong Yacht Club for ten years and Commodore for two years. He is also a member of the Hong Kong Sailing Federation and the Water Sports Council. Most weekends, he takes part in competitive sailing. In July 2015, the government appointed him a member of the Harborfront Commission, of which he continues to be a member. "With giant container ships, there is less traffic in the harbor. I am happy to see it more used for leisure, recreation and water sports," he said.

EUROPEANS IN HONG KONG

On December 27, 2020, Hans Dieter Isler passed away in Salzburg, Austria. Since 1954, he had maintained his primary home in Hong Kong. He was a founding member of the German Chamber of Commerce and was actively involved in establishing and running the German Swiss International School. For this, he was awarded the Order of Merit of the Federal Republic of Germany.

Learning German

To learn German, Hong Kong people go to the Goethe-Institut Hongkong (香港歌德學院). It was founded in February 1963 in Caxton House, Duddell Street in Central. German-language courses began in August that year and attracted 900 students in the first year. In the same year, the Goethe-Institut organized its first musical events. The Hong Kong Arts Center opened in 1977. In 1978, the Goethe-Institut moved into the 13th and 14th floors of the center; that has been its permanent home since then. Its mission is to promote German language and culture, foster cultural cooperation and provide a center of information on life, politics and society in Germany.

About 6,000 people a year attend the Goethe-Institut's language courses for adults, teenagers and children. Since 1964, more than 40,000 students have enrolled its courses and taken one of its international exams. Many of them work in German companies or want to study and work in Germany. Nevertheless, the majority of the Goethe-Institut students learn German because they have a personal interest in the language and culture. Among the German learners at the Goethe-Institut are regularly journalists, creative people and leading cultural managers of various institutions—in short, interesting people with whom it is fun to be in a German course. Currently about 2,500 Hong Kong people are living in Germany, many of whom learned German at the Goethe-Institut, including the well-known blogger Chui Kit Lam, who reports about life in Germany on the Goethe-Institut website.

For two years now, the Goethe-Institut has also been offering courses for children and young people aged from five to twelve years, for which there is a growing demand. Every year in autumn, the Goethe-Institut organizes its Open Day with an entertaining program for young and old German learners and those interested in Germany and the German culture.

In collaboration with schools and universities in Hong Kong, the Goethe-Institut runs educational projects to promote German as a school and study subject. In the framework of the initiative of the Federal Foreign Ministry of Germany, "PASCH—Schools: Partners for the Future", it supports two schools in Hong Kong where German is taught as a regular subject; four more schools offering German to primary and secondary students participate in projects and receive up-to-date German teaching materials. Together with five Hong Kong universities and the consulates general of German-speaking countries, the Goethe-Institut runs the Inter-university German Language Olympics every two years. In collaboration with the European cultural institutes in Hong Kong, the EU office of Hong Kong and Macau and the Consulates General of European countries it organizes the "Speak Dating Event" to celebrate the European Language Day every year.

Furthermore, the Goethe-Institut Hongkong regularly offers teachers' training for German as a foreign language and provides students and teachers with scholarships for study trips to Germany.

The Goethe-Institut library, which is open to the public and free of charge, has around 7,000 items, including 700 feature and documentary films in German with English subtitles. Besides its physical library, its digital library Onleihe is also accessible to the public. The Goethe Library also serves as a meeting point for activities and events organized for its students and the general public. For example, German authors and library experts are invited to Hong Kong to host talks and workshops on a regular basis. And with its latest focus on 'digital offers', the library also strives to provide its users with the interesting technological experience through events such as 3D printing workshops and Virtual Reality Weekends.

Each year Goethe-Institut Hongkong organizes a wide variety of cultural programs, including an annual festival of German films, KINO, with twenty-four to twenty-six screenings in the autumn; concerts and other performances; and exhibitions by German, Hong Kong and international artists. Recent major projects include the 100 Years Bauhaus anniversary in 2019, with exhibitions, films, conferences and workshops, celebrating the legacy of the world's most influential school of art, architecture and design, and the Projekt Berlin, a festival of music, media art, cinema and street art, from and about one of the world's most exciting metropoles, Berlin. With the Goethe Gallery, for a long time one of the very few non-commercial art spaces in Hong Kong, the Goethe-Institut has been nurturing the next generation of local artists as well as introducing German and international artists, bringing inspiring new trends to Hong Kong. The Goethe-Institut has been building bridges between the art scenes in Hong Kong and Germany through residency programs, such as the Hong Kong-Berlin residency program for filmmakers by fostering innovative co-productions like the CONTAIN.er project by Hong Kong New Music Ensemble and Ensemble Resonanz, Hamburg. It invites German musicians, artists, film directors, authors and experts in various fields to Hong Kong. It also invites local art practitioners to Germany, to attend festivals like the Tanzplattform and the Berlinale, to conduct performances, give concerts or engage in collaborations. For more than five decades, the Goethe-Institut has been developing a strong and trusting network with all major art institutions and festivals in Hong Kong, as well as with universities, museums, libraries and independent artists.

The Goethe-Institut in Germany was established in 1951, just six years after the end of World War II, with the mission to spread knowledge about Germany by providing information on its culture, society and politics. This includes the exchange of films, music, theater and literature. Goethe cultural societies, reading rooms, and exam and language centers have played a role in the cultural and educational policies of Germany for more than sixty years. Today, there are 157 Goethe-Instituts in ninety-eight countries, including twelve in Germany, with 270,000 attending its language courses and 550,000 taking its internationally recognized examination each year. The Goethe-Institut has been an important part of the country's soft power, rebuilding its reputation after the tragedy of the war.

According to its website, "it sets internationally recognized standards in the teaching and learning of German as a foreign language. It runs language courses, compiles teaching materials, trains teachers, monitors trends in Germany and encourages cultural collaboration across the globe by organizing programs of events and making contributions to various festivals and exhibitions in the fields of film, dance, music, theater, literature and translation. Libraries and information centers, forums for discussion, diverse print-, audio- and video-publications and our visitors' service aim to paint a contemporary portrait of Germany, promoting international discourse on the key concerns of what is becoming an increasingly global society."

The Goethe-Institut is mainly financed by the national

government of Germany. It has around 3,650 employees worldwide and an overall budget of €408 million euros, about one third of it from language course tuition and examination fees. It also receives contributions from sponsors, patrons, partners and friends that enable it to broaden the scope of its work.

Dr Almuth Meyer-Zollitsch has been director of Goethe-Institut Hongkong since December 2016. She says, "Hong Kong is a fascinating metropolis, with a multi-faceted, highly professional cultural scene. The Hong Kong people are proud of their own identity, their Lion Rock spirit, but at the same time open to other cultures, new encounters. This is certainly connected to the fact that Hong Kong itself was created by migration, by a constant inflow and outflow of people. Hong Kong people like to travel a lot, it's in their DNA, so to speak, and they like to learn languages. Perfect conditions for a cultural institute like the Goethe-Institut!"

The German Swiss International School (德國瑞士國国際學校) opened in 1969 and now has 1,300 students from over thirty countries. It is a multi-language school operating two parallel streams and teaching two curriculums, from kindergarten to secondary school, and prepares for the German International Abitur (GIA) and the International Baccalaureate (IB), following IGCSE examinations in Year 11. Its aim is to produce students who are trilingual, in German, English and either Mandarin or French.

The school was born when a small number of Swiss and German parents in Hong Kong came together with the aim of setting up a German-language school from kindergarten to secondary level. They were led by Gunther and Ingrid Buchholtz. It was their foresight in the early 1960s that eventually led to the opening of the school in rented premises on 1 Barker Road on the Peak. By the summer of 1969, 130 children had registered;

in October, the school opened under the leadership of Ingrid Buchholtz. The oldest child was 10, the youngest 4. At first, the school fees were HK$50 per month for kindergarten and HK$100 for everyone else. A kindergarten teacher received HK$600-800 per month, the Principal worked for nothing, and unmarried teachers were accommodated with families. The Buchholtzs chose the building despite the fact that it had been vacant for a long time, because of rumors that it was haunted by ghosts. After World War II, the Dutch Consul General who lived there had fallen seriously ill.

Ghosts or not, the school flourished. Lessons were in English and German with the intention that children would grow up fluent in both languages. In September 1970, at the start of the school's second year, 201 children were enrolled and registration had to be restricted. By September 1972, the number had reached 362 and there was a long waiting list. The building on Barker Road was too small.

In response, the government provided free land. In 1973, construction of a new school building on Guildford Road began to accommodate increasing student numbers. In 1975, the new building on Guildford Road — now Upper Building — opened; it has become the permanent home of GSIS.

Since then, the school has continued to expand. In 1989, student numbers surpassed 1,000. It now has Primary, Middle and Upper Buildings on the Guildford Road sites. In 2008, the school Building Committee began to plan a second school campus in Pokfulam for the kindergarten and lower primary; it opened in August 2010. Then came construction of new facilities on the main campus, including an indoor swimming pool, a senior library, a black-box drama studio, a primary gymnasium, the Three Mackerels Cafeteria, a school shop and IT rooms.

GSIS works to create a welcoming and vibrant environment

where students from the German International Stream (GIS) and English International Stream (EIS) play, interact, and learn from each other. In an interview in May 2020, Principal Ulrich Weghoff said, "As we have students from such a diverse background—Chinese, local and German students—represented in both streams, they are thoroughly exposed to the various cultures, religions and languages. In the process, they have effectively cultivated an open mind and independent thinking." The school organizes learning opportunities for students outside of the classroom, with field trips, assemblies and cultural events. "As Germany is Hong Kong's largest trading partner in the EU, the cultural integration between Hong Kong and Germany is all the more meaningful," he said.

"Bilingualism is pivotal in the globalized world. Past research has shown that bilingual students, compared to monolinguals, score higher in their academic achievements, not to mention the bonus advantage of language proficiency that opens up opportunities to study, live and work in different parts of the world. Our students in both streams are deeply articulate, creative, outward-looking young people with an impressively strong set of academic results. In both streams, we have a consistently high level of achievement with progression to top universities around the world. We value the diversity of our community and, with more than countries being represented at our school, we embrace the myriad of perspectives this brings."

In its kindergarten, the school runs the Fast Track Program—an intensive German-learning experience designed for students with little to no prior knowledge of German to integrate into the GSIS community, and embark on the GIS in grade K06. To help the acquisition of German as a second language, the program has dedicated German-language courses that are integrated into the normal timetable, alongside German students, to cultivate a language-rich learning environment. There is German-language immersion in PE, Music and Arts and use of bilingual education in Sciences and Social Sciences. In other subjects where the curriculum is more language-based, such as History and Geography, there is an additional teacher who gives support where needed. Weghoff said their programs stood the students in good stead to apply for top-ranking colleges and universities in the United States, Canada, the United Kingdom and Europe. Grit Cichon, head of the German International Stream, said that the GIA curriculum covered other languages as Mandarin, Latin and French. "We understand and address the changing learning needs of our students as they progress on their learning journey," she said. German vies with French as the second language of Europe, after English. It has an estimated eighty million German speakers, including the residents of Germany, Austria and most of Switzerland, as well as countries of Eastern Europe, where German is often the second language.

Entry into GSIS, as into other international schools, is not cheap. The parents of each successful applicant must pay a debenture. "As a registered non-profit organization, GSIS depends on tuition fees and government subsidies to finance the school's operational costs," it says on its website. "GSIS recognizes that, over time, existing facilities will need enhancements, additions and replacement to maintain and continue to improve the overall school environment for our students. GSIS's debenture scheme was conceived to meet the cost of major capital projects and provide for the sustainability of GSIS into the future." The parents choose one of two options — a refundable debenture of HK$500,000 when their child enters the school and which is returned when he or she leaves, or a 'development debenture' of HK$432,250, which is not returned when the student leaves and becomes a donation for its future capital development. The school fees for the 2019/2020 year ranged from HK$156,110 for kindergarten to HK$203,420 for secondary school.

The school has a longstanding policy to consider social aspects of students attending the school on a case-by-case basis, particularly for German, Swiss and Austrian nationals and their children. For them, attendance at the German Stream of GSIS is the only way of receiving an education similar to that of their home countries. Reduction of school fees is possible for qualified applicants, determined by a means test.

Famous Photographer
The work of German photographer Michael Wolf is well known both to Hong Kongers and also internationally. His photographs portray the density of living here, his up-close public housing facades, his work on the residents of a Shek Kip Mei estate. Then there are those where he used to love wandering down the back alleys of Hong Kong — pink rubber gloves pegged on hangers, with a mop and broom alongside; umbrellas; a bamboo chair, years old, faded, fixed with string.

Later in life, his work also encompassed sunrises — meditation in the early morning, a free horizon. All his work shows his love for a city that he made his home — and kept returning to even when he left — for twenty years. It's a beautiful legacy left by Michael Wolf, who died in 2019 at the age of sixty-four. On occasion, he would head off to Tokyo, Chicago and Paris, but was drawn back by the energy of the metropolis he portrayed so uniquely.

"Michael was an exuberant, curious character who just wanted to explore, which comes across in his work. He was always running around the back alleys or photographing even if it wasn't with his camera. He'd use his phone or make a video," says Jonny Davies, the director at Flowers Gallery in

Sheung Wan. Davies knew Wolf for a number of years and in 2020 "Spotlight on Michael Wolf" was the inaugural exhibition of Flowers Gallery, when it opened in Sheung Wan.

"He would engage with the people around him," says Davies, describing how in addition to his photography, Wolf amassed a collection of old chairs with plastic ties, lovingly and economically repaired over the years. Wolf would ask if he could have the chair for his collection and then buy the chair owner a new one.

"He was a great storyteller, whether it be through his pictures or in person. He loved to tell stories. And that was one of the most captivating things about him and spending time with him," says Davies.

Wolf was born in Munich, southern Germany in 1954, but spent his childhood until he was 19 years old in the United States and Canada. He attended the University of California, Berkeley. He studied photography at the Folkwangschule of Essen in Germany and studied with Otto Steinert, one of the most significant German photographers of the post-war period.

In 1994, Wolf came to Hong Kong to work as a photojournalist for the German magazine, *Stern*, which he did for eight years before moving into his own projects. These included "The Real Toy Story" — a collection of around 20,000 toys made in China but bought in California and stuck on the wall of a gallery. There was also "100 x 100" where, using a wide-angle lens, he shot the frugal homes in a Shek Kip Mei public housing estate that was about to be demolished.

Several bodies of work — "Architecture of Density" and "Tokyo Compression" were about city living. But Wolf also chose to shoot tower blocks during a distinct period in Hong Kong's recent history when there were fewer people around.

"It was around 2003 around the time of SARS that Michael

started photographing industrial buildings and large blocks of flats where people lived in so densely. And there was an element that not many people were around at the time so they were a bit more empty," says Davies.

Wolf also photographed Hong Kong's corner houses—blocks often six stories or fewer with rounded façades and often painted in pastels. Usually more than fifty or sixty years old in Hong Kong's fast-changing urban landscape, many of the corner houses have disappeared over time.

The quirky, artistic photographs of his "Informal Solutions" series are described by Flowers Gallery as "a series of photographic typologies and vernacular sculptures that show an intimate perspective of the city from within its hidden network of back alleys". Wolf would use a mix of equipment—a more formal camera, but sometimes his iPhone or iPhone video. And while his photographs of those rubber gloves, a bamboo pole, and hangers with pegs have a distinct artistic resonance, he never actually moved any of the items to suit his composition, says Davies.

"His work was all about the density of living from the architectural series to the back alleys," says Davies. "It was then juxtaposed from his move to Cheung Chau, which is where he then started this series of the "Cheung Chau sunrises". So, he'd wake up each morning and take these pictures. It was almost a therapeutic body of work or series that he was taking. He meditated a lot and woke up early and I now see it as a therapeutic way of him capturing something which was the antithesis to his urban density. He really did love that island. And it was his peaceful place that he went to."

Chapter Two
The French

In the early years of Hong Kong, the French business community was not as large or powerful as that of Germany. In 1862, the first French bank, Comptoir d'Escompte de Paris (巴黎國民貼現銀行), opened an agency in Hong Kong. But it, and other French banks that followed, found it hard to compete with the powerful British banks that had close relations with the colonial government and the Chinese business community here and in the Mainland. In 1881, HSBC opened an agency in Lyon (里昂), center of France's silk making industry that bought raw material from China; the business flourished for many decades. One of the most important French companies was Messageries Maritimes (法蘭西火輪船公司), a shipping line that business in 1866; it was the only French firm able to compete with the major shipping lines in cargo and passengers. For many decades, it was the most important link between the mother country and the community here. In the first quarter of the 20th Century, the journey from Marseille (馬賽) to Hong Kong took twenty-nine days, bringing passengers, cargo, mail and news; a ship arrived every fifteen days. One of its most luxurious liners was the Félix Roussel (菲利克斯・魯賽爾

EUROPEANS IN HONG KONG

號), built in the St Nazaire shipyard in 1930; it served the Far East from 1930 to 1955. It was 171 meters long and could carry 4,000 passengers.

A French bacteriologist made a major contribution to Hong Kong by identifying the bacillus that devastated Hong Kong in 1894. Between May and October, it killed more than 2,000 people and a third of the population fled the city. It was one of the most serious public health disasters in its history. On June 22 that year, Alexandre Yersin, 31, made his discovery. One year later, Yersin worked with colleagues at the Pasteur Institute in Paris to develop a serum that was successfully tested on a plague patient in Hong Kong in 1896. It was the first anti-plague serum. To honor him, the bacillus is named Yersinia pestis.

What is more remarkable is that Yersin made the discovery working in a bamboo hut built at his own expense near the Kennedy Town Hospital, the main center for fighting the disease. The research team there was led by Japanese Professor Shibasaburo Kitasato; the hospital managers rejected the request of this young Frenchman they did not know for facilities similar to those of the Japanese researcher. But he was able to find the help of an Italian priest, Father Bernardo Vigano, who acted as his guide and interpreter. As a military chaplain, Father Vigano knew soldiers and sailors in the British Army. Yersin bribed some of them, who were guarding the mortuary, to give him corpses on which he performed autopsies. Since he had no oven or refrigerator, he kept his samples at room temperature. Most of the dead were Chinese living in crowded and unhygienic conditions in the district around Tai Ping Shan street; dozens of rats in the area were also dying. This led Yersin to deduce that the bacillus also infested rodents and that the rat flea carried it to humans. Both he and Kitasato did autopsies and experimented with mice, rats and guinea pigs. The Japanese professor was a meticulous researcher; on June 20, 1894, he announced that he had discovered the bacillus. Two days later, Yersin made public his findings. They were formally announced at the Academy of Sciences in Paris on July 30 and his paper on the plague published in the Annales de l'Institut Pasteur later that year. While the results of the two men were similar, the medical world concluded that Yersin's conclusion was correct — and therefore named the bacillus after him. His discovery had profound significance for the residents of Hong Kong; 2,500 of them died of the plague by the end of 1894. The serum was available after 1896.

Yersin was born on September 22, 1863, in Aubonne, in the Vaud canton of Switzerland, where his father was a professor of natural sciences. Yersin received his education in Lausanne and Marbourg in Germany. In 1885, he moved to France, where he joined the Pasteur Institute, one of the foremost medical research institutes in the world, especially in the fight against infectious disease. Yersin studied under its founder Louis Pasteur; he researched rabies and tuberculosis. With a colleague, he discovered the toxin that causes diphtheria. In 1889, he obtained French nationality. In character, Yersin was shy, timid and solitary. Perhaps that is what drove him to leave France and travel in its colony of Vietnam in 1890; he fell in love with the country. He took a job as a doctor with a shipping company, which went from Saigon to Haiphong and Manila. He used the time to learn Vietnamese and explore the country's rivers and forests. He settled in Nha Trang, a seaside town 300 kilometers north of Saigon. In 1895, he established there a branch of the Pasteur Institute, which he equipped with the material needed to research the plague. It was named the Pasteur Institute by the French government which sent him to Hong Kong to study the plague.

After Hong Kong, he spent the rest of his life in Nha Trang. In

1902, he founded a medical school in Hanoi. He persuaded the colonial government to develop a town nearby his home; this became Dalat, a center of sanatoria and large colonial villas. He set up a secondary school in the town and helped to develop its farms and forests. He was made an Officer of the Legion of Honor in 1939. He died at his home in Nha Trang on February 28, 1943, aged 79. At his funeral, an enormous crowd followed the coffin, wishing to honor his contributions to Vietnam. His house is now a museum and he is remembered today, with a street named after him in Ho Chi Minh City, where nearly all the street names are Vietnamese. His time in Hong Kong was short, but his contribution to medical science significant.

Missionary Contribution
For the first century of Hong Kong, the greatest French contribution was that of the missionaries. In March 1847, Father Napoleon Libois, Procurator General in the Far East of the Society of Foreign Missions of Paris (MEP), relocated from Macao to Hong Kong. In 1848, he moved into his new headquarters at 6 Staunton Road, which would be his home and office. This French organization was one of the largest missionary orders in Europe. The next year a second French order arrived. On September 12, 1848, three French and one English nun arrived in Hong Kong after a perilous four-month journey by sea from France. It marked the start of one of the most important religious missions in the city that continues until today. The four were members of the Sisters of St Paul de Chartres (the Sisters).

The Society of the Paris Foreign Missions (in French, Société des Missions Etrangères de Paris (MEP) 巴黎外方傳教會) was the first French order to come to Hong Kong. It was established in 1663, to conduct missionary work in foreign lands. In the 350 years since then, it has sent more than 4,200 priests to Asia,

Canada and the Indian Ocean; developing a local clergy has always been one of its main objectives. It remains active today in evangelizing Asia, with 180 priests, fifteen seminarians and 150 volunteers sent each year to Asia and countries around the Indian Ocean.

By mid-19th Century, MEP had sent missionaries to many parts of Asia, including Vietnam, Korea, Japan, Tibet, Burma, Malaysia and China. In several countries, including Japan, Korea and China, proselytizing was illegal. Missionaries had to work underground; some were arrested, tortured and killed, as were those they converted. Bishop Gabriel-Taurin Dufresse was martyred in Sichuan in 1815. In Vietnam and Korea, missionaries could only be sent illegally; sometimes they could only enter on pirate boats. So the establishment of a British colony in China, controlled by a pro-Christian government that would protect missionaries, was an excellent opportunity. In March 1847, the MEP's Procurator General in the Far East, Father Napoleon Libois (李播), relocated from Macao to Hong Kong. In 1848, he moved into his new headquarters at 6 Staunton Road. It was not only to be his home and office; but it also had to be large enough to accommodate the many missionaries who would come through Hong Kong and wait there, sometimes for months, before going to their posts. Father Libois' main duty was to welcome these missionaries and guide them to their posts. He oversaw the enormous proselytization work of Japan, Korea, China, Burma, Laos, Malaya and Vietnam; he had branches of the MEP in Singapore and Shanghai. He managed the large amount of funds donated by Catholics in France to spread the faith overseas. Father Libois stayed in Hong Kong until 1866 and welcomed a total of more than 220 new missionaries; half of them went to China. Of these, twenty-four were violently killed during their mission or en route. In 1984, Pope John Paul II canonized ten for

Korea: in 1988, ten for Vietnam: and, in 2000, three for China. During a British-French military expedition to China in 1860, Father Libois provided two MEP priests as interpreters and one as a Navy chaplain.

In 1866, he was succeeded as General Procurator by Father Pierre-Marie Osouf. He continued the work of Father Libois — caring for the young missionaries and sending them on their way to their posts in East Asia. Many fell sick and came to Hong Kong for rest and recuperation; but the mission house was not large enough to accommodate them all. So Father Osouf proposed construction of a sanatorium where priests in the Far East could be treated for tropical diseases and given spiritual support; they could regain their strength before returning to their missions. After obtaining approval from his superiors in Paris, the Father purchased for HK$3,000 twenty-four hectares of pristine farmland on a hill next to the new Pokfulam reservoir; it was 139 Pok Fu Lam Road, with a large garden overlooking the sea. The cost of the land and building was covered by a year's income from the reserve fund of the MEP's Hong Kong Procure. The sanatorium, with a chapel, opened in 1875; named Bethanie, it had fourteen well-appointed bedrooms, each with a study, and a veranda with spectacular views of the South China Sea. It welcomed its first sick missionaries on October 4 that year. The fathers created a beautiful garden and a path down the steep hill, so the patients could bathe in the sea. In the early years, the skills of its medical staff could not save all the patients, especially those suffering from tuberculosis, for which there was no cure. Over time, medical technology greatly improved. During its 100 years of service, it treated an average of more than sixty missionaries a year; 101 of them died there.

Printing Center for Asia

In 1894, the fathers acquired Douglas Castle, a nearby building, and spent two years converting it into their printing center for Asia, named Nazareth. They had already started printing books in 1884 in Macao and Hong Kong since 1885, but on a smaller scale. They used Nazareth to publish religious books, dictionaries and other scholarly works in twenty-two languages, including Chinese, Korean, Japanese, Vietnamese, Siamese, Khmer, Laotian and Tibetan, as well as European languages. Books in some Asian languages had never been printed before. Between 1884 and 1934, Nazareth printed more than three million copies, an average of 62,000 copies and twenty-nine editions a year. Its books were sold all over the world, especially to Asian communities. During World War II, the whole community left for Saigon, except for two fathers who stayed behind to look after the printing press. Fortunately, it was not damaged by the Japanese. It resumed work in 1948.

During World War II, Japanese troops ransacked Bethanie and expelled the missionaries. They took all the furniture, destroyed the bathrooms and ripped out the electrical system. Short of fuel, the troops cut down the 50-year-old coniferous trees in the garden, leaving it bare. After the Japanese surrender in 1945, the Hong Kong government occupied the sanatorium as a hostel. It was only in May 1950 that the fathers were able to receive sick missionaries again. It was especially busy in the two years after 1949, when the new Mainland government expelled all foreign missionaries. During those two years, Bethanie treated seventy missionaries; they stayed for a total of 4,950 days. During the next two decades, air travel improved and the MEP permitted its missionaries to take leave in France every six years, instead of eight and ten previously. So the need for a sanatorium in Hong Kong diminished.

EUROPEANS IN HONG KONG

In 1974, the MEP sold Bethanie to Hongkong Land. But the company found the site too difficult to develop and exchanged it with the government for land elsewhere. In 1981, Bethanie was declared a Grade II listed building; it was used by Hong Kong University. In March 2003, the Legislative Council approved funds for the Hong Kong Academy for Performing Arts (HKAPA) to restore the building and two cowsheds nearby that belonged to Dairy Farm. The project took three years and cost HK$80 million. The result today is a site with six different elements—a museum of the MEP's work in Asia for 300 years, a chapel in regular use, a 150-seat theater, a seventy-seat screening room, a school of film and television, and a multi-function studio.

In 1903, the MEP appointed a new Procurator General in Hong Kong, Father Leon Robert (金羅拔). Born on March 24, 1866, he had been sent to the colony in 1888, aged 22, to work as Assistant Procurator. He served three years until 1891, before spending twelve years as Procurator in Shanghai. He was an unusual priest—he was also an investor, a developer and counselor of the government of the French Concession. It was a critical period of China's history—the devastating loss to the Japanese in the 1894-95 war and the Hundred Days Reform (戊戌變法) in Beijing in 1898 which ended in failure. Father Robert published a newspaper L'Echo de Chine; it had local and world news in French and was published until July 1927. He became an adviser to his government of the fast-moving changes in the last years of the Qing dynasty. He served in Hong Kong from 1903 until 1926. It was a time of rapid growth of the MEP. In 1882, the MEP was in charge of twenty-five missions, with 641 missionaries, 394 local priests and 783,000 Catholics. By 1912, it had thirty-four missions, with 1,394 missionaries, 889 local priests and 1.55 million Catholics. Father Robert was in charge of managing this 'empire' in different countries of Asia. It reached into many regions of China and often operated among hostile rulers and populations. It meant that he was better informed about Asia than the majority of diplomats, scholars and journalists in Hong Kong and China.

Hong Kong provided the perfect platform for his business acumen in the service of the MEP. From 1905-1907 and from 1914-26, he was on the board of the *South China Morning Post* (南華早報), the city's leading English-language newspaper then as now. He bought shares in the paper which the MEP retained for nearly sixty years. Considering the high rentals of its Connaught Road offices wasteful, he urged purchase of a property in North Point; but the procrastination of his fellow directors and his tough negotiating style caused the plan to fail. In 1970, the newspaper did make such a move. If it had followed Father Robert's wise advice, it would have saved millions of dollars. He also bought many shares in Hong Kong and Shanghai Bank (HSBC) and attended its shareholder meetings. He was on the board of several companies, including Dairy Farm and Hong Kong Land. He actively managed the large share portfolio of the MEP, which included China Provident, Hong Kong Hotel Company, Hong Kong Land and Lane Crawford. The substantial income from this portfolio helped to pay for the MEP's operations all over Asia, mainly in China.

Father Robert built a wide network of connections with the business community in Hong Kong, including Sir Catchick Paul Chater, one of its leading entrepreneurs. All this meant that he was extremely well informed; he used these connections to teach people through Catholic education and the media. In 1914 in Hong Kong, he chaired the first conference on Catholic schools and the Press in China. He used his influence to protect the interests of Catholic schools and other institutions. After the outbreak of World War I, Governor Sir Henry May thought of him to manage all the charity institutions run by the Germans, but he refused and forwarded the request to the Catholic Mission of Hong Kong. While the Hong Kong government welcomed the Catholic Church, its senior officials were Protestant; and the city had a strong and vocal Protestant community. The government of his own country, France, was anti-clerical. In July 1904, it broke diplomatic relations with the Vatican; in 1905, it introduced laws against the church. So Father Robert had to be nimble and persuasive to look after the interests of MEP across Asia.

Father Robert was also active in real estate. In 1915, he bought 1 Battery Path and rebuilt it; the work took twenty-one months and the MEP moved in early in 1919. The building later became known as the French Mission Building. His connections also enabled him to help the Sisters of St Paul find their new headquarters in Causeway Bay; we describe this in the following section on the Sisters.

His primary duty was to his MEP colleagues. In 1921, for example, his headquarters received 220 members of the order, as well as 112 other priests. He received decorations from the Republic of China and from France. In 1921, he was elected First Assistant of the Superior-General; he remained in Hong Kong, since it was better to have one member of the leadership team in Asia, in the days before Airbus and Boeing. He left Hong Kong in 1926. In 1928, he embarked on a long journey to visit the missions and settled in Paris in 1929. In March 1935, he was elected Superior General of the MEP, a position he held until 1946. In 1937, he made another long visit to the missions in the Far East, returning to France on the Trans-Siberian railway in 1937. In October that year, he received the honor of L'Officier de la Legion d'Honneur. In November 1945, he retired. He died on October 15, 1956, at the age of ninety. His funeral was attended by ten bishops and senior figures from French civil society; he is buried in the Montparnasse Cemetery in Paris.

Father Robert was succeeded as Procurator-General by Father Leon Vircondelet. He was born in 1890 in Vesoul, Haute Saone in eastern France. His first posting was Guangzhou. In 1921, he was sent to Hong Kong as assistant to Father Robert and took over from him after he returned to France. He too was active in business and managing the MEP investments. He bought and sold properties in Yaumatei, Prince Edward Road, Tokwawan, Sookanpo and elsewhere. An official document in 1952 said that MEP earned more than HK$600,000 a year from shares and HK$35,000 a month in rents from its properties, of which it had built 90 percent itself.

The Japanese occupation was a Calvary for the MEP and Father Vircondelet, as it was for everyone in Hong Kong. The Japanese took over one of its three buildings, but not the Battery Path site, which they considered a place of worship because of its chapel. During the war, it was used by many people, including the Irish Jesuits, the Tonkin Coal Company and the French Consulate General.

The French nation and people were divided between the Vichy government, established in July 1940, and the Free French government in exile in London, led by Charles De Gaulle. The Vichy regime worked with Nazi Germany and its ally Japan. French overseas, such as Father Vircondelet, had to decide to which side they belonged. He chose the Free French side. He worked hard to protect the assets and interests of the religious orders and prevent looting of their properties, especially the Nazareth printing work. He assisted many French residents in the city, including Consul General Louis Reynaud. When Reynaud died in 1943, Father Vircondelet moved the consulate into the Battery Path building, in order to preserve a symbolic presence for his country.

EUROPEANS IN HONG KONG

After the war, he worked hard to repair and reconstruct the buildings of religious orders that had been badly damaged. The Hong Kong government took over two of the MEP buildings as temporary hostels. It was only in August 1948 that it returned the Battery Path building to him. In 1948, he organized celebrations for the 100 years of the Sisters of St Paul in Hong Kong. That year the French government awarded him the Legion of Honor in recognition of his work during the war.

In 1949, the communist government took power in China and expelled all foreign missionaries. This posed an enormous challenge to Father Vircondelet. Suddenly, hundreds of MEP missionaries arrived in Hong Kong, some in poor health. It was his task to look after them. China's revolution meant a profound change for the society; the main purpose of its operation in Hong Kong was to support its priests in China, financially, materially and in other ways. But they could no longer be able to operate there. A mission of thousands of Fathers and Chinese priests trained by them over more than a century had come to an abrupt end.

In 1952, Father Vircondelet decided to sell the imposing building on 1 Battery Path to the Hong Kong government for HK$2.85 million. From 1997 to 2015, it was the first home of the Court of Final Appeal; in September 2015, the court moved to the Old Supreme Court building in Central. In 1954, he also sold Nazareth House to the University of Hong Kong for HK$1.5 million. It became the University Hall that remains in use today. This sale was not welcomed by all the members of the MEP; its printing presses were providing books and materials badly needed by the church across Asia. Probably fearful of a communist takeover, Father Vircondelet also sold many properties in Hong Kong.

In 1960, Father Vircondelet retired. He remained in Hong Kong for a further ten years. He left finally in 1970, after living here for forty-nine years, and went to a retirement home in Montbeton in the Tarn et Garonne department of southern France. He died there in November 1973.

Some of the MEP fathers expelled from China settled in Hong Kong and became priests of parishes here. This was the first time in the mission's 100-year history that they had held such posts. One was Father René Chevalier (明之剛 神父). Born in Beaupreau in Maine-et-Loire in March 1909, he was ordained a priest in Paris in 1942. In May 1946, he was assigned to the Sheklong leper house in Guangzhou. He ministered to the lepers and learned Cantonese. In July 1952, he was expelled, ending his six years of service to the lepers. He was appointed parish priest of Taikoolao (太古樓) in Pokfulam, serving forty families whose fathers had worked at the Nazareth printing press. Taikoolao was a complex of staff hostel, primary school and chapel built by the MEP. All its residents were Catholic. Father Chevalier had a car that he used to visit the members of his congregation; there was no public transport in the area at that time. He allowed his parishioners to drive it when they wished. One day in 1952, he drove a young woman to hospital where she gave birth to a boy. The baby grew to become Father Dominic Chan Chi-ming (陳志明); he was Vicar General of the Hong Kong Diocese from December 1992 to January 2019. He was one of three priests and four sisters to come from the Taikoolao community. In 1958, Father Chevalier founded the Our Lady of Lourdes Kindergarten in Lamma Island; it is thriving today. Usually smoking a pipe, he regularly visited hospitals and orphanages. He also visited a center for tuberculosis patients in his parish; many had been abandoned by their families. He maintained contact with the priests and Catholics he had known in Guangzhou — but never spoke about them.

EUROPEANS IN HONG KONG

In 1971, the parishioners in Taikoolao had grown to 1,800. That year Father Chevalier was transferred to the Holy Spirit Seminary in Aberdeen, as spiritual director. In April 1981, he went to visit his nephew, a missionary in Thailand, and see the refugee camps there. On April 23, on his way back from one of these camps, he was killed in a car accident. On May 4, more than 1,000 people, including John Wu (胡振中), Bishop of Hong Kong, and 100 priests, attended his funeral at the Chapel of the Sisters of St Paul of Chartres. In his eulogy, Father Dominic Chan said that, when he told his parents of his wish to become a priest, they objected. "They feared that people would mock us, saying that we wish to profit from the Church. Father Chevalier went to see them and explained the situation. He encouraged them not to let their son miss this opportunity. It is thanks to him that I became a priest...We must do all we can to continue his service, especially to those old people who have been abandoned and have no voice." The Father spent thirty-five years of his life in China, twenty-nine of them in Hong Kong.

Another parish priest in Hong Kong was Father Joseph Marius Madéore (戴天恩神父). He was born on February 7, 1901, in Billom, Puy de Dome. After ordination at the MEP chapel in Paris in May 1926, he was sent to work in Guangxi Province (廣西省). From 1937 to 1952, he worked as a missionary in the Nanning (南寧) diocese. In 1947, he was appointed Vicar General of the diocese. On September 1, 1952, he was expelled from China. He arrived in Hong Kong and built from nothing the parish of Kennedy Town; its population soared with the arrival of refugees from the Mainland. The Father rented a first-floor flat in a crowded tenement building and turned it into a Rosary Chapel. Helped by a group of volunteers, he provided a daily distribution of rice and fresh food. On March 1, 1957, the district became the Parish of Our Lady of the Rosary, with 1,000 members. Within six years, the congregation grew from 150 to 3,000.

By 1963, the parish had a church on Pokfield Road (蒲飛路), a school, a presbytery, meeting rooms and offices. Father Madeore retired in 1973, at the age of seventy-two. He settled in Hong Kong, where he passed away on December 20, 1981, aged eighty. Two bishops, twenty priests and many of his parishioners attended the funeral in the church he had built. Other MEP priests in Hong Kong worked in the pastoral field, with young people, refugees, Filipinos, hospital patients and the resident French community. Between 1847 and 2020, 105 MEP priests stayed in Hong Kong, working on its projects here or in parishes. Others came only for medical treatment or taking rest and recuperation; more than 100 are buried here, at least ninety-nine in Chaiwan Cemetery and four in the Happy Valley Cemetery.

According to the MEP website, fourteen members of the society work today in China, the majority in Hong Kong. Four are undergoing training and one senior member is retired. The others work in pastoral care—celebrating the sacraments: training young people, especially in Catholic schools, and baptizing many every year: visiting old people and those in hospital: training small Catholic communities: historical and theological research. Some Mandarin-speaking priests live and work in Taipei, where they have close ties with the local dioceses.

Sisters of St Paul—Schools and Hospitals

The second French religious order to come to Hong Kong was the Sisters of St Paul de Chartres (the Sisters, 沙爾德聖保祿女修會). On September 12, 1848, three French sisters and one English one arrived in Hong Kong after a perilous four-month journey by sea from France. It marked the start of one of the most important religious missions in the city that continues until today. The

EUROPEANS IN HONG KONG

Sisters have left an enduring legacy today—a kindergarten, two nursery schools, two primary schools, three secondary schools, one nursing school, two hospitals, an orphanage, a chapel, a convent and House of Prayer, a novitiate for training nuns and St Margaret's Parish, Happy Valley. The schools educate more than 6,000 children; the hospitals have 1,568 beds and provide state-of-the art medical care. The graduates include many of the city's most prominent citizens, such as Dame Lydia Dunn, Anson Chan, Doreen Kwok Le Pichon, Margaret Ng, Ann Hui and Christine Loh.

Initially, the Sisters came from France, Belgium and Britain. The first Chinese sister joined in 1862 and the first Chinese Provincial Superior was appointed in 1968. The last French Sister, Marie Auguste Roue, passed away in Hong Kong on March 9, 2001, having lived in the city for seventy-two years. Today there are seventy-one Sisters, including Chinese, Koreans, Vietnamese and Filipinas. They have sent missionaries to Taiwan, Australia, where they run a hospital, a boarding school and a retirement home, and to Myanmar. They ventured to the Mainland in 1899 until their withdrawal in 1949 after the communist takeover. In 1996, they also went again, discreetly, to the Mainland, where Korean missionaries ministered to the Korean Catholic community in Beijing until 1999, when the mission was transferred to South Korea.

The Sisters of St Paul de Chartres was founded in 1696; it is one of the oldest female missionary orders. Its mission was to educate the very poor, particularly young girls, and care for the sick. Its first foreign mission was to Madéore in 1727. Between 1792 and 1811, it was, like other religious orders, suppressed during the French Revolution. In 1818, the Sisters went to Martinique and, in 1820, to Guadeloupe. The mission to Hong Kong was its fourth overseas. On December 14, 1847, Monsignor Theodore

Augustin Forcade, Pro-prefect Apostolic of Hong Kong, wrote to the Reverend Mother General. He asked her to send Sisters to Hong Kong to set up an orphanage to raise abandoned infants, nearly all of them girls.

> *Letter of Msgr Forcade:*
> *"I would need Sisters to run the hospital for the Irish soldiers. I would need Sisters to run the school for their daughters ...*
> *Finally, I would need Sisters to run an already established small hospital to bring up those little Chinese abandoned by their parents.*
> *What else? I would perhaps even need Sisters to train ... young Chinese, who will later on take up the responsibility of running hospitals and schools for their own people."*

She gladly accepted the request. It was the first foreign religious women congregation to come to Hong Kong.

On October 1, 1848, the four sisters in Hong Kong received their first infant. By the end of the year, they had accepted 170; three quarters of them were close to death. Not all survived, but all were baptized. Within two years, the Congregation in Hong Kong had its first martyr. Sister Alphonsine, one of the original four and the Superior, contracted cerebral fever and died on October 11, 1850; she was just thirty-seven. She was buried in Happy Valley Cemetery in the section reserved for the religious. Just three weeks later, another of the original four, Sister Gabrielle, also died; she was only thirty-three. Between 1848 and 1854, the Sisters accepted 1,360 abandoned children — an astonishing figure, given that Hong Kong's population was less than 25,000. If the Sisters had not accepted the girls, they would have been left to die or sold as servants or concubines.

The Mother House sent three more sisters from France. In 1851, the Sisters moved to bigger quarters in Wanchai and called it Asile de la Sainte-Enfant (Refuge of the Holy Child), after the Association of the Holy Childhood in France, which provided the funds. Monsignor Forcade encouraged the Sisters to encourage local vocations and train local people to provide educational and social services. Between 1848 and 1897, the Sisters baptized 34,113 abandoned babies, of whom 88 percent were female. They fed and clothed these orphans, taught them reading, writing, religion and sewing; at a proper age, they arranged for them marriage with good Catholic men. New buildings in 1872 and 1893 allowed accommodation of hundreds more orphans; many were adopted by local and foreign couples. They raised money for this work from Chinese Christians and received donations from Catholics in France, gave private French lessons, and sold the lace and needlework made by the orphans.

On November 1 1876, Mere Paul de la Croix Biard opened a school, forerunner of the present St Paul's Convent School in Causeway Bay. By the end of the century, it had two sections - French and English. From the beginning, there was a section for the Chinese orphans; in 1925, they opened this section to the public, and two years later opened a branch in Happy Valley. In 1931, they added additional classes, including a higher class of Middle School.

During the plague of 1894, the Sisters accepted dozens of elderly women who asked for shelter. This became a hospice for handicapped and old women. The plague persuaded the Sisters that they needed to build a hospital. So, on January 1, 1898, the dispensary became St Paul's Hospital, where 2,000 patients were treated every year. At that time, health care for the general public was a low priority in the government's agenda; it focused on public health and disease prevention. Those who wanted hospital treatment had to rely on charitable organizations, including religious ones and traditional Chinese institutions. Most doctors of western medicine were foreigners or Chinese who had graduated overseas; nearly all of them were in private practise and charged high fees. The inauguration of the hospital took place in 1898. On the first floor, 36 elderly women were accommodated, with the number later rising to 60. The second floor served as a shelter for the Sisters of the Assumption who were forced to leave their establishment in Manila during the Spanish-American war. After the exiles were repatriated, Mother Felicie put their rooms at the disposition of the Chinese ladies to look after themselves or to care for their little children under the guidance of the Sisters. Two German doctors performed surgeries—Dr Karl Justi, the hospital's Medical Attendant, and Dr Oskar Muller. There were no fixed charges; each patient gave as he wished and his purse allowed. The Sisters provided nursing services and a caring role.

In the early decades of Hong Kong, most Chinese regarded Western medicine—with its foreign doctors, knives, needles and anesthetics—with suspicion. Chinese doctors of traditional medicine were cheaper and more available. The plague of 1894, which killed more than 2,500 people, changed the minds of many people. Traditional medicine was helpless in treating the disease; only western methods were effective.

In 1908, Governor Sir Frederick Lugard opened an annex for the Sisters in Happy Valley, Le Calvaire, a hospice for the needy and a refuge for the poorest. By 1914, the Sisters owned two plots on the sea front in Wanchai. It included a convent, a small hospital, a boarding school for young girls, a workshop, a hospice and a novitiate. These premises became too small for the demands put on them. The area had become too crowded and too noisy. Trams ran under the windows of the hospital until midnight each day and there were several brothels nearby. They urgently needed new premises.

New Hospital

The Sisters were aided in their search for a hospital by Father Leon Robert, Procurator General of the MEP in Hong Kong from 1903 to 1926, whom we mentioned in the previous section. In mid-March 1914, through his contacts in the business community, he learned that Jardine, Matheson wanted to sell its large cotton mill in Causeway Bay and move its operations to Shanghai. It was 400 feet long and 110 feet wide, with large windows. He visited the site; on this first viewing, he decided that, after renovation, it would be an ideal place for the Sisters. On March 26, he wrote a detailed letter to the Superior General of the Congregation, with designs of the plot, the alterations he proposed and financial projections. He proposed financing it by the sale of the Wanchai properties to Sir Catchick Paul Chater, one of Hong Kong's wealthiest entrepreneurs and a personal friend. On June 22, the Superior General telegraphed her agreement. The project cost in total HK$640,000 and involved major renovations to turn the mill into what the Sisters needed –a convent and chapel, an orphanage, a workshop and a hospice, a boarding school, a European and Chinese hospital. It was a major conversion project; there were no new buildings, but conversion of existing one. Most of the school buildings were made of wood. World War I complicated the building work, which began on November 1, 1914. The Sisters took over their new orphanage on October 6, 1915, the convent in January 1916 and the boarding school in October 1916. Governor Sir Henry May opened the convent school on October 6, 1916. The project was finally completed on May 15, 1918, with the opening of the hospital, with three stories. It had a state-of-the-art operating theater and luxurious private rooms together with standard rooms which the poor could afford. Eight French and two Chinese Sisters and four Filipino nurses provided nursing care. The operating theater was one of the most advanced in Hong Kong, costing HK$30,000 and including two equipment rooms. The hospital had a maternity section, general ward, isolation room, consultation rooms, dispensary, and X-ray room. The price for a first-class room was HK$7 per day, for a second-class one HK$4-5 and for a third-class one, with four beds, HK$0.5-1.0. There were also beds for those who could not pay and a clinic for poor Chinese run by an elderly Sister, who had been in Hong Kong for thirty-five years. There was also a car park and a mortuary. The project was profitable—Father Robert sold the Wanchai land for HK$321,000 and Mother Ste Felicie Jourdan, the Provincial Superior in Hong Kong, had set aside US$100,000. By 1923, the Sisters had repaid the debts. Father Robert wrote, "We could have economized a lot by using cheaper building materials, and by doing things more simply. This would have been a bad plan in Hong Kong. The people are willing to pay but want to be at ease, the reason why the school and the hospital, with some luxury, were immediately well appreciated by the people."

In 1915, the Sisters took over a large, three-story property on a small hill thirty meters southeast of the new site. This had previously been a reformatory for boys and then a refuge for destitute women; it was run by a German superintendent and other German staff. In 1914, they had to leave Hong Kong because of World War I. The next year, the government asked the Sisters to take over the management. They continued the valuable, unobtrusive work for the rehabilitation of women and girls; they also utilized St Paul's Refuge as a laundry to handle the enormous load of cleaning required by the hospital. They used it for the next seventeen years until 1932, when the government took back the building for other uses. The Sisters then built a laundry within the St Paul's Institution.

After the successful move to the new compound, Mother Felicie and Father Robert began to plan construction of a large chapel in the middle of the compound. It aimed to serve the 800 people who worked in the different parts of the compound. Included in the original plan, the project was suspended due to a lack of funds. Then a Hong Kong architect, Joseph Chan A Tong (陳納堂), stepped forward; a devout Catholic, he had put up several buildings for the Sisters in Causeway Bay. He offered to design the chapel at no cost. The foundation stone was laid in 1928 and the new chapel consecrated on May 10, 1930, with six bishops and forty priests co-celebrating. Unfortunately, Mother Felicie passed away in 1926; she handed the project to her successor, Mother Marguerite de St Paul Nuss. Christ the King Chapel is one of the largest and most beautiful churches in Hong Kong, with space for 1,000 people. French artists sculpted the high altar in Carrara marble; it weighed seventeen tonnes. They exhibited it in Paris for two months before shipping it to Hong Kong. It was a gift from donors. The concrete platform on which it stands had to be reinforced to carry its weight. Initially, the chapel was only for the private use of the Sisters. They made certain exceptions. As more and more people requested to use it, the Sisters have permitted the public to celebrate the Eucharist there on Sundays. But, since it is a private chapel, it does not host weddings. It is widely used today.

Over a century later, the hospital is still operating on the site—evidence of the wisdom of the decision taken by Father Robert and the Superior General. The hospital is popularly known as the French Hospital (法國醫院). Today it has 470 beds, including a six-story wing added in 1975 but demolished in 2011 to construct a new block, Block B, as well as an extension

(Block A) [22] completed in 2009. Upon completion of the two blocks, the original building, the last vestige of the old cotton mill, was pulled down. On the opening of the hospital, Father Robert consulted with the Sisters in Hong Kong. He advised the Superior General in Chartres to send capable nuns to run the school and hospital; on arrival, they should learn English and Cantonese. But France had a strongly anti-clerical government. In 1904, it had banned religious orders from engaging in education and closed Catholic schools. As a result, the Sisters had over the next ten to twelve years, sixty-seven percent fewer vocations.

In 1936, the Sisters acquired a bungalow in Kowloon for an orphanage; they turned part of it into a clinic. The population of the area was growing rapidly and needed medical care. On behalf of the Sisters, Father Vircondelet, Procurator General of MEP, purchased land at 327 Prince Edward Road, where they built St Teresa's Hospital. It opened in 1940, with three stories and seventy-five beds; it received its first patient on September 14 that year. Like its sister in Causeway Bay, it was and is popularly known as the French Hospital (法國醫院). From a small hospital, it has developed into a 1,098-bed medical center with advanced facilities and equipment, surpassing those of St Paul's Hospital. It was Sister Bernard de Marie de Broqueville who spearheaded the gradual transformation of the hospital in 1959. Granddaughter of the former Belgian Prime Minister Count Charles de Broqueville, she became Hong Kong's last foreign missionary Provincial Superior in 1960, initiating sweeping beneficial administrative changes in the running of the Province.

World War II was a tragedy for the Sisters as it was for the rest of Hong Kong. The Causeway Bay compound was in the middle of a military area, surrounded by arsenals, warehouses, oil tanks and training camps. After the Japanese invasion on December 8, 1941, the area was hit by more than 200 shells from the Japanese and British armies. Only the chapel and part of the hospital were unscathed. After the British surrender on Christmas Day 1941, the Japanese took over Le Calvaire in Happy Valley and St Teresa's Hospital in Kowloon. Here is a report on St Paul's Hospital at that time:

"In December 1941, the hospital having been seriously damaged, we had to evacuate it and place the Sisters in the Convent, while the patients were transferred to the Anglo-French School, the classes being closed since the beginning of the bombardment of Hong Kong on December 8, 1941. Two large rooms in the Orphanage were prepared to receive the wounded. Since these two rooms are not always full, and now they are always occupied by poor patients."

The Japanese detained all but three European doctors and nurses and sent them to a detention camp in Stanley. It sent Chinese nurses to replace the British ones; only Chinese civilians could be received in the hospital.

The Japanese took over the hospice in Happy Valley; the Sisters and their charges were moved to Causeway Bay. The compound there became a military headquarters and prison. In Causeway Bay, there were so many sick and wounded that the school and orphanage became part of the hospital. Classrooms were turned into operating theaters; the chapel was also used to treat the many wounded. The population of the hospital compound rose to 500 to 600. During the war, the chaplain of the hospital, convent and orphanage was Father Richard Gallagher, an Irish Jesuit who was not detained by the Japanese because of his nationality—Ireland was neutral during the war. Life was difficult and dangerous; everything was in shortage. Every day was a battle for survival.

On April 4, 1945, American bombers mistakenly dropped fourteen bombs on the convent school and orphanage; they killed fifty-four orphans and six Sisters. Eight of the nine buildings of the compound were damaged. The orphanage and buildings for the blind and disabled were entirely destroyed. Only the chapel and main wing of the hospital were spared. It was Father Leon Vircondelet of MEP who looked after the children and Sisters. He sent some of the survivors to Macao where they took refuge until the end of the war. The Canossian Sisters in Hong Kong kindly came to their rescue and generously sheltered and cared for some Sisters and orphans. Fr Vircondelet then organized a team of 200 volunteers to clear the ruins and reconstruct the damaged buildings. The Sisters returned and continued their work. St Teresa's Hospital reopened in late 1945, as did St Paul's Hospital and the educational establishments. In 1949, a maternity wing, Pavilion Notre Dame, was added at St Paul's Hospital to provide more maternity services. In July 1949, the first of the Filipina missionaries arrived to make up for the loss of foreign Sisters during and after the war.

The communist revolution in China transformed Hong Kong. The Catholic population of the city tripled from 50,000 in 1950 to 150,000 in 1960. Tens of thousands of refugees arrived. Mother Bernard was actively involved in providing much needed relief and assistance to these refugees. The Sisters opened new missions and took over two schools to cater to their needs. In Tai Po, they opened a kindergarten as well as a clinic and the parish Sacred Heart of Mary Primary School; in Kennedy Town, a primary school and a clinic; in Tai Hang Road, a clinic that was closed in 1968 as well as the one in Kennedy Town. In 1970, they opened a third Paulinian secondary school in Lam Tin, a refugee resettlement area. With the arrival of this new labor force, the economy developed rapidly and many women went out to work; the size of families dropped and the number of orphans fell. In 1964, the Sisters changed the nursery and orphanage in

Causeway Bay into a nursery school. After World War II, the number of religious vocations in France, as in other European countries, fell. The Sisters needed to recruit elsewhere. In 1968, the Congregation appointed its first Chinese Provincial Superior, Mother Marie Isabelle Tc; she served until 1978. In 1975, they completed St Paul's Convent in Causeway Bay as the seat of administration, retirement home and infirmary for old, retired and sick sisters; it has its own chapel and places for those on retreat. At the end of the 1970s, with the lack of qualified Sisters, the Province returned the administration of two primary schools to the Taipo and Kennedy Town parishes of Hong Kong. During the 1980s, the old school buildings in Causeway Bay were redeveloped.

The approach of the city's return to China in 1997 was a big challenge to the Catholic community. Fearful of rule under the Communist Party, thousands of Catholics decided to emigrate. It became more difficult to recruit young women to join the Congregation. In 1996, the Sisters handed supervision of the two hospitals to Professor Sir Harry Fang and Dr Christina Chow. Both were highly respected in the medical community.

In 1998, the Sisters held celebrations to mark the 150th anniversary of their arrival in Hong Kong. In April, they organized a Thanksgiving Anniversary Mass, Jubilee Night and Anniversary Dinner. In attendance were the Superior General, Reverend Mother Anne-Marie Audet from France and Provincial Superiors of Vietnam, Japan, Korea, Thailand and the Philippines, countries which traced their origin from the first missionary journey in 1848. Also in attendance were one hundred orphans who had been raised by the Sisters; they and their families were invited to a dinner after a Eucharistic Celebration. Later that year, St Paul's Hospital celebrated its centenary. Taking part in the opening ceremony were Chief Executive Tung Chee Wah

(董建華特首), Cardinal John Baptist Wu (胡振中樞機), Bishop Joseph Zen (陳日君主教) and Bishop John Tong Hon (湯漢主教). On March 9, 2001, the last French Sister passed away, aged ninety-seven. Sister Marie Auguste Roue had lived in Hong Kong for seventy-two years since her arrival in 1929. She worked in St Teresa's and St Paul's Hospitals. She served as Superior of St Paul's from 1971 to 1974. The Sisters held a Mass of Resurrection for her on March 14, 2001, at the Christ the King Chapel. The aging of Sisters coupled with the lack of new vocations to replace them has greatly affected the nature of the mission. To address this problem, the Hong Kong Province has vigorously sought to import young blood to augment the depleting number of Sisters in Hong Kong. It turned to Vietnam Province, which is at present enjoying a boom in religious vocation, for assistance. An addition of twenty young Vietnamese missionaries since 2004 has been a shot in the arm for the aging and ailing population of sisters in Hong Kong. Unlike previous missionaries, they are 'made in Hong Kong' so to speak, except for a few already professed sisters, as they, arriving as candidates, received their religious formation in Hong Kong after studying Cantonese for two years.

The Sisters today continue the legacy inherited from and passed on by the French and other missionaries, albeit in different ways, but with the same apostolic zeal and devotion. Aside from the education and healthcare ministry, the Sisters also carry out apostolic, pastoral, charitable, and social works. School Pastoral Workers and Hospital Pastoral Teams fulfil their mission and apostolic goals in schools and hospitals. By organizing various activities, they help create a religious atmosphere and culture, to provide students with opportunities to grow in their faith. In the hospitals, they minister to the spiritual needs of the staff and patients. The hospitals also provide financial assistance by way of low-cost beds, discounts and fee waivers. They have outreach programs, like free health checks, medical missions extended to the local community as far as the Mainland, as well as distribution of basic necessities to the needy. Sisters teach catechism and prepare candidates for baptism and confirmation in parishes. They also minister and provide assistance to ethnic minority groups, such as the Vietnamese community and Filipino and Indonesian overseas workers, according to their particular needs. Apostolic and social works are carried out by a Service Support Committee, which serves disadvantaged and vulnerable groups like refugees and migrants by volunteering and conducting private lessons, Chinese and interest classes.

On November 29, 2011, a new community, Our Lady of Chartres Community, was opened. Located above the new STH School of Nursing building just across St Teresa's Hospital, it is another residential place for Sisters working at the hospital. On September 8, 2018, three Sisters were installed at Greenfield Community, Sheung Wan, a venue for charitable projects, such as after-school tuition class, tutorial groups, and so on, as well as residential units for students or individuals with special needs. Another housing project near St Teresa's Hospital provides affordable lodging, while a subsidized Geriatric Ward was opened in 2013.

The Province has also launched three re-development projects. The St Paul's Hospital re-development project started in 2006; two blocks were completed to enable it to operate by 2017. Construction of two new school buildings are underway — the St Paul's Primary Catholic School in Happy Valley and St Paul's Catholic Day Nursery in Taipo.

Camembert, Culture and Engineers
The earliest French arrivals were priests and nuns. Today they are active in all sectors of life, including manufacture, trading,

retail, finance, luxury goods, high-tech, education, medicine, music and the arts, food and wine. They are the single largest single European community in Hong Kong, numbering 25,000. It is the second biggest French community in an Asian city, after Singapore. More than 800 French companies are based there; 373 are subsidiaries and ninety-two are regional headquarters. Every year since 1993, French May has presented more than 150 programs over two months, including film, food, exhibitions and performances. It has become an iconic part of Hong Kong's cultural scene that reaches out to more than one million visitors each year. It is one of the biggest festivals of French culture outside the mother country. In addition, there has been a French film festival in the city every November since 1972. Hong Kong is and has been one of the most important windows for French products and culture in Asia.

During the two World Wars, France was an ally of Britain, so its citizens here were able to continue their life and work here, unlike the Germans. This chapter describes the French contribution in Hong Kong to education, publishing, business, medicine, art and haute cuisine from World War I until the present day.

Director of Schools
In 1914, a French priest named Brother Aimar Sauron (艾瑪・撒隆), a member of the De La Salle order, arrived in Hong Kong. Born in 1873 in Cévennes (塞文山脉), south central France, Aimar Sauron worked for fifty-two years as a missionary teacher in the Far East, in Singapore, Penang and then Hong Kong. In 1914, he was appointed director of St Joseph's College, one of the most important secondary schools in the city. During World War I, the government confiscated the imposing German Club on Kennedy Road and gave it to his order. In September 1918,

St Joseph's moved in and has remained there ever since. The number of students increased; those who had to make the long journey from Kowloon asked if the school could open a second site there. Brother Aimar embraced this project. On April 23, 1928, he purchased ten acres of land on Boundary Street at public auction for HK$120,000. St John Baptist de la Salle School opened on January 6, 1932, with twenty classrooms, an assembly room and laboratories for physics and chemistry. By 1939, there were 1,060 students, with, in addition, a full-size football pitch and four tennis courts. Brother Aimar also purchased three acres nearby; the La Salle Primary School was later built there. He remained an outstanding head of the school until the Japanese occupation. He fled to Indochina and died on November 5, 1945, at the Brothers' Formation House in Nha Trang, Vietnam. In 1966, his ashes were returned to Hong Kong and buried under his bust in the hall of the college. It remains there today, in La Salle Road, one of the best secondary schools in the city. It is the legacy of Brother Aimar to his adopted home, where he is lovingly remembered by old boys of the school.

Rebel Consul

World War II was a nightmare for the small French community in Hong Kong, as it was for their compatriots around the world. In June 1940, their country fell to the Nazis and a collaborationist government was established under Marshal Philippe Petain. Members of the French administration, at home and abroad, had to swear allegiance to the new regime, if they wanted to keep their jobs and salaries. Louis Reynaud (路易·雷樂), consul in Hong Kong, refused. Aged fifty-six, he had been in the city for two years, with a thirty-six-year-long diplomatic career behind him; fluent in Chinese, he was strongly pro-British. On June 20, he sent a telegram to his superiors in Paris saying, "Gathered around me, the French colony of Hong Kong rejects any idea of armistice and separate peace. It is revolted at the thought of such a betrayal in front of our allies and mankind."

It was just two days after the famous radio broadcast from London by General Charles de Gaulle calling on his countrymen to resist. As a result of his attitude, Reynaud was ostracized from the diplomatic service, cut off from confidential messages and no longer received a salary. After the Japanese occupied Hong Kong, they closed all the consulates in March 1942. Reynaud succeeded in obtaining the permission of the new rulers to remain in the city as a private citizen. He was able to draw his pension; he continued to use both the consul's office and official residence, to prevent their being looted. He used his personal savings to support seventeen members of the French community, mostly women and children. Exhausted and discouraged, he died in the French Hospital in Causeway Bay on July 6, 1943. After their victory, the Japanese encouraged French families to move to the French colony of Indochina and deported others to camps there. There were about seventy French citizens living in the city outside the camps in October 1942.

More than forty French people joined the Hong Kong Volunteer Defense Corps and took part in the defense of the city against the Japanese invaders in December 1941. They took part in the fighting until the surrender on Christmas Day. Two were killed during the battle: one died in an internment camp in Hong Kong, another in an internment camp in Japan. One killed himself by jumping out of the window of a police station after being tortured by the Japanese military police. One survived internment but died on December 29, 1947, in Hong Kong, weakened by his experience. On March 31 1948, a stele in memory of these six Free French was inaugurated at the Stanley Military Cemetery by Consul Robert Jobez (饒伯澤).

The monument has been restored and inaugurated in December 2019. Five new names were added, following recent historical research, taking the number to eleven.

Frenchman Henri Vetch was the first head of Hong Kong University Press (HKUP), which was established in 1956. He had an extraordinary life, as a soldier, scholar and publisher; he spent most of it in China. He was born on December 2, 1898, in La Celle Saint-Cloud in the Yvelines department outside Paris. From 1900 to 1906, he lived with three elder brothers in Fuzhou. His father worked there as a commission agent recruiting Chinese workers for Madagascar and the French colonies in the Indian Ocean. After his parent's divorce in 1907, Henri was brought up by his grandparents in the Seychelles. In 1917, he returned to France to join the French Army. In 1920, he went to Tianjin to join his father who was running La Libraire Francaise. Then he acquired the French Bookshop in the Grand Hotel de Pekin. In the 1930s, he established a reputation as bookseller and publisher. He produced books on different aspects of China in English, Chinese and other languages written by well-known Western authors and Sinologists. His bookshop was both an academic club and private library; it played an active role in the cultural life of Beijing. Vetch was a knowledgeable and lively conversationalist; many scholars came to his shop. In 1939 to 1941, he again served with the French Army in Indochina. In 1941, he returned to Beijing and lived through the communist revolution.

In September 1950, he was arrested with six other foreign residents and accused of espionage and a plot to assassinate Mao Zedong . In August 1951, a court martial in Beijing announced the death sentence of the two "ringleaders", an Italian merchant and a Japanese man who worked as Vetch's assistant in his bookshop. They were the first death sentences pronounced on foreigners since the foundation of the PRC. The trial was not public, the prisoners were not allowed to meet anyone, including their families, or present evidence. The two were executed. The other five were sentenced to prison. Vetch was given ten years and served three, before being deported in April 1954. Vetch was probably saved from a death sentence by his French nationality; his country was a member of the United Nations Security Council, while the countries of the two who were executed were on the losing side in World War II. Vetch served his sentence in two prisons in Beijing, including a period of solitary confinement. He was permitted to read the complete works of Shakespeare, which his daughter Helene later said kept him from going mad. He also used the time in prison to learn Chinese, which he had scarcely spoken before. The official press said the seven were working for the Office of Strategic Services (OSS) of the United States and planned to use mortar shells to kill Mao on the reviewing platform of Tiananmen Square on October 1, 1950, during a parade to celebrate the first anniversary of the new state. It said that the mastermind behind the plot was David Barrett, former US military attaché in Beijing.

The US State Department called the accusations "crude lies". The consensus opinion at that time was that the charges were fabricated and that the trial and sentences, well publicized in official media, aimed to intimidate Chinese into having no contact with foreigners. In September 1954, the government allowed Henri's wife Elena to leave Beijing and join her husband in Hong Kong.

In 1956, he founded Hong Kong University Press and guided it through its difficult early years; he was strongly supported by Vice Chancellor Lindsay Ride. He published scholarly books similar to those he had produced at the company he had previously managed in Beijing and had earned him an international reputation. In 1956, it published six books, including *The Castle of*

EUROPEANS IN HONG KONG

Indolence by James Thomson *and Chronological Studies of the Pre-Ts'in Philosophers* (先秦諸子擊年) in Chinese, by Qian Mu (錢穆), with a forward in English. In 1957, it published four books, including *Robert Morrison, the Scholar and the Man*, by Lindsay Ride, the Vice Chancellor of the University. Morrison was the first Protestant missionary to China. In 1968, his final year at HKUP, it published four books, including *"Revolution in Siam 1688: the Memoir of Father de Beze"* and a translation of Chao Lun (肇論), The Treatises of Seng-Chao (僧肇). These titles illustrate the range of Vetch's interests and scholarship.

In 1968, Vetch retired and set up Vetch and Lee, a new publishing company in Queen's Road Central. His partner was Rupert Lee, founder of the Swindon Book Company. Vetch died in Queen Mary Hospital in Hong Kong on June 3, 1978. His daughter Helene took his ashes back to France. After her mother died, she placed them within her mother's coffin. In an obituary in The *Times* newspaper on July 6, 1978, Sir Cohn Crowe, a former British diplomat who had served in China between the wars, described Vetch as "a man of immense erudition and scholarship with a wide knowledge and love of Chinese culture. He was an extremely good businessman and bookseller. He was well known to all with his lanky figure, untidy mop of gray hair and bubbling enthusiasm."

Today HKUP is publishing fifty books a year from leading scholars around the world. In total, it has published more than 1,000 titles. Most of its books, especially academic books, are in English, with a minority in Chinese. It has authors in North America, Europe and Asia, making it a global publisher. The subjects include law, education, social work, medicine, real estate and construction. "We are also committed to a full line of books on linguistics and language study, including making Chinese in all its varieties more available to English speakers and making English more accessible for Chinese speakers," it says on its website.

After World War II, French people returned to Hong Kong. Some were businessmen who had lived and worked, often for many years, in the colony of Indochina. In 1954, the French army lost the war against the Viet Minh, leading to the creation of the communist state of North Vietnam and a pro-American state in the south.

Emile Kleber Texier, a former French military officer in Shanghai, had spent eighteen months in Japanese prisons in Guangdong. After settling in Vietnam, he left in 1957 and moved to Hong Kong. He first worked as a representative for Ford Simca Motors (西姆卡); after it went bankrupt, he became a tourist guide because of his excellent knowledge of the city and fluency in Cantonese. Some French business people became sourcing agents for large European firms, buying the many goods which Hong Kong was starting to manufacture. Others provided components, equipment and raw materials to the manufacturers. In the 1980s, a growing number of French multinationals opened offices in Hong Kong; many used it as a base for their China and regional operations. By the end of the 1980s, there were 275 French companies in Hong Kong, more than four times the sixty-seven in the Mainland. They included large retail chains like Carrefour (家樂福), Leclerc (勒克萊爾) and Casino (卡西諾). As the economy of the Mainland boomed with that of Hong Kong, so the number of French companies increased; they were in many sectors, including law, banking, logistics, interior decoration, hotels, water treatment and industrial goods. The French Chamber of Commerce and Industry in Hong Kong (香港法國工商總會) was founded in 1986; by 2019, it had 933 members and thirty dedicated staff, making it the fifth-largest French chamber in the world. One third were non-French speakers.

EUROPEANS IN HONG KONG

In 2015, it set up the French Chamber Foundation (法國商會慈善基金) as a charity; it operates four centers in the city to help low-income people improve their livelihoods, through training and job-matching. The four also provide low-cost meals. In the financial year that ended June 30, 2019, the foundation helped 800 disadvantaged people and provided 44,077 low-cost meals. At a gala dinner, the Chamber raised HK$1.7 million for the Foundation.

Two major engineering firms have made important contributions to the city. In 1955, the colonial government asked Societe Francaise de Dragages et Travaux Publics (Dragages寶嘉) to build a two-kilometer runway for Kai Tak airport. The firm accepted the offer; it took twenty months of work and moving 8.5 million cubic meters of rock to construct the runway into the harbor. It also worked with Soletanche (法國地基建築公司), another French company, in building the Shek Pik Dam on Lantau Island, creating a large freshwater reservoir. Over the next decades, the two companies took part in many infrastructure projects, including the Lion Rock tunnel, the Plover Cove Dam, the MTR and the Aberdeen Tunnel. Dragages also helped to build Hong Kong Park, the new Hong Kong Stadium, Happy Valley Racecourse and AsiaWorld Expo. Bachy Soletanche has completed more than fifty major projects in the city, mainly underground. They include the foundations of the HSBC headquarters, AIA Central, Times Square and the International Commerce Center.

The residence of the Consul General was a beautiful European-style home in the Mid-Levels, with large grounds behind it. It had previously been the residence of the Colonial Secretary. By the end of the 1970s, it had become too expensive to maintain. In 1983, the French government sold the property for HK$120 million, a record at that time. It used the money to buy two villas on the Peak, for the consul and the deputy consul, a dozen apartments and two floors in Admiralty for the consulate's offices. It also used HK$5 million of the money to build a permanent home for the French International School (法國國際學校). As a result, France has since then owned all its consular offices in Hong Kong, a blessing in the world's most expensive property market. In 2011, it sold the residence on the Peak for HK$580 million, another record.

Initially, producers of French luxury goods were represented by Hong Kong companies and sold in department stores and boutique chains owned by local families. From the 1970s, the producers began to open their own operations in the city, with offices and outlets. Louis Vuitton (路易威登) opened its first boutique in Hong Kong in 1979 and now has ten, all in upmarket locations popular with tourists. Since the 2000s, Mainland Chinese have fallen in love with French luxury goods, including accessories, watches, jewelry, beauty products, perfume and cosmetics. These visitors now account for about eighty per cent of the customers of luxury boutiques in Hong Kong.

French food and wine have always been popular in Hong Kong. In the 1970s and 1980s, cognac was indispensable on the menu at high-level banquets where wealthy Chinese from Hong Kong or the Mainland were invited. Cognac was a symbol of 'face' and success. The price of a bottle in Beijing reached US$1,000. A popular advertizing jingle of Remy Martin (人頭馬) at that time was "人頭馬一開，好事自然來" ("Rentouma Yi Kai, Haoshi Ziran Lai—Open a bottle of Remy Martin, Good Things Always Follow"). Famous French chefs came to the city and opened high-end restaurants. Companies imported high-end French food for sale to hotels, restaurants and supermarkets. One of the biggest employers of French people is the wine industry. The French consulate, the French Chamber of Commerce and other wine-producing countries lobbied the SAR government to abolish duties on wine. In 2008, it did so—to dramatic effect. In 2008 and 2009, 850 new wine-related companies opened in the city, taking the total to 3,550; the number of people working in wine-related businesses increased by more than 5,000 to nearly 40,000 by the end of 2009. Ten years on, imports of wine have tripled since 2007, making Hong Kong the top importer in Asia, ahead of Tokyo and Singapore. According to figures from the Hong Kong Trade Development Council, imports in the January-June 2019 period were HK$4.5 billion, compared to HK$1.6 billion for all of 2007; the volume in the six-month period was 21.9 million liters, of which 24 percent was re-exported and the rest taken out by individuals leaving the SAR or retained for storage or local consumption. Of the imports, 81.8 percent came from Europe, with 63.9 percent from France, far ahead of Britain in second place, with 10.2 percent cent. The Mainland is the main export market from Hong Kong, which has become the main distribution center for Asia. The Hong Kong Trade Development Council forecast annual wine sales in the Mainland rising 4.1 percent by value and 1.1 percent by volume between 2019 and 2023. The abolition of duties has proved to be a bonanza for French wine producers and professionals, including managers, teachers and sommeliers. Jeremy Stockman, general manager of Watson's Wine, said in November 2018, "From a trade point of view, Hong Kong is the place to be for wine. Back in 2008, if you wanted to be in wine, you were in London, New York, maybe Tokyo. If you want to be in wine today, you come to Hong Kong. Just take a look at all the young French people who are here in the wine industry. People come here to be involved. That encourages the wine culture." In 2007, the first local edition of the Michelin Guide (米芝蓮指南) was published in Hong Kong.

A man who has witnessed—and helped to create—the

transformation of the diet of Chinese is Jacques Boissier. He arrived in Hong Kong in 1993 to run the Asian division of a large French trading firm. In January 1, 2001, he set up Classic Fine Foods to import high-quality foods from Europe and sell them to customers in Asia. "Twenty years ago, Chinese did not drink wine or eat expensive meat or dairy products. All this has changed. Now they eat better, they drink less and better," he said. "The word 'retire' is not in my dictionary. I have bought an apartment here and plan to stay. My friends, Chinese and Western, are here, my life is here."

Boissier had an international childhood few in the world can match. He was born in 1953 in Paris to a family whose origins are in Berry, in central France. His father worked for Air France. When he was three, his father was posted to Kenya for five years. Next came Tokyo, for another five years. "In 1963, when I was ten, I came to Hong Kong for the first time, from Tokyo. I was overwhelmed." During three of his parent's five years in Japan, he stayed in France, to attend school there. Then came five years in London, where he passed his baccalaureate. "My father told me to be open to the world, be fluent in English and develop my curiosity. I was very fortunate to have such opportunities in my childhood." The only downside was that, since he changed schools so often, he had no school friends. "I did not make friends until I was 23 and started my professional life." He went to university in Reims, where he graduated in 1973.

After graduation, he went to work for La Societe Commerciale de l'Ouest Africain (SCOA), a French conglomerate founded in 1907 with interests in many sectors of the economy in West Africa. He worked for three years in Gabon in information technology. Then he moved to Nigeria, the biggest country in the region for SCOA. There he ran IT for the group for ten years. In 1993, the company sent him to Hong Kong to manage the

Asian operations of Olivier, an import-export firm founded in 1847. In 1875, it started operations in Shanghai, then in Tianjin and Hankou. It later opened offices in Hong Kong and Tokyo. When Boissier took charge, the main activities of the firm were food, clothes and wine. "These were all new sectors to me, I had to learn everything. The company's operations in Asia were in decline, I had to restructure it." In 1995, the firm was sold to Bernard Arnault, France's richest man and chief executive of LVMH Moet Hennessy, the world's largest luxury goods company. He bought Olivier in his personal capacity and asked Boissier to stay on as manager. In 1998, Arnault sold the firm to Veuve Clicquot Champagne.

On January 1, 2001, Boissier embarked on a new adventure, with the foundation of Classic Fine Foods (CFF), based in Hong Kong. He was the minority shareholder, with the majority held by the Vestey Group, a British company with international operations in meat and refrigerated products. A gourmet, Boissier adapted easily to this new field. CFF imports high-quality food, from Europe, Australia and New Zealand and sells them to customers in Asia and the Middle East. "We sell only high-level, famous brands, always with an exclusive contract," he said. Its customers include five star hotels and restaurants, airlines, supermarket chains and delicatessen stores. Its products include caviar, foie gras, wagyu beef, Iberico ham and brand chocolates, as well as dairy, other meats, pastry, seafood, condiments, pasta and dry products. Its Hong Kong headquarters is in a logistics center in Kwai Chung. "We have 100,000 square meters of warehouse, with four different temperatures. You must protect the cold chain." Its catalogue contains more than 3,000 items. "At the start, we employed twenty people. Now I have 190 people working for me, 165 in Hong Kong and twenty-five in Macao."

He said that twenty-five years ago, Chinese did not eat cheese.

"We started with sliced cheese that had no taste, which people consumed for their calcium. Now Chinese eat cheese with strong and refined tastes. Twenty-five years ago, Chinese did not drink wine. It was beer and Mao Tai (a potent sorghum liquor). Then they started to drink cognac, and then wine. It started with red, then white and now rose. Before, Chinese women did not drink; now they do." For three years, Boissier was involved in a joint venture in Tianjin with three partners. One was a Scottish whisky firm (Glenfiddich), one an Argentine wine company and one a Chinese-state firm that made rice liquor. CFF was responsible for distribution. "We provided all kinds of drinks to banquets. Chinese drink less and better. They eat better. There has been a westernization of the diet. Chinese have traveled widely in Europe and it is a fashion to try western food. Habits have changed—people want organic food, they want wellness and to be able to follow the food chain. They want to know where it was produced, what it contains and whether it is safe." Boissier talks constantly to chefs to find out the latest trends and what food they are preparing.

The corporate structure of CFF has changed. After seven years, the Vestey Group sold its stake to EQT, a private equity firm. In August 2015, Dusseldorf-based retail giant METRO GROUP bought a 100 per cent stake. "The transaction covers the operations and all fixed assets of CFF for an enterprise value of US$290 million plus an earn-out of up to US$38 million depending on the EBITDA [Earnings before interest, taxes, depreciation and amortization] performance in 2015 to 2017," METRO said in a statement at the time. It said CFF (Classic Fine Foods) covered twenty-five cities, mainly Asian, in fourteen countries, employed 800 people, had annual sales of more than US$200 million and was highly profitable. Now Boissier is responsible for the markets in Hong Kong and Macao. "Since the

EUROPEANS IN HONG KONG

takeover, the company is more structured, with a chief executive. But we remain very entrepreneurial."

Bossier praised the business environment of Hong Kong. "It possesses a unique system that helps entrepreneurs, creating companies and the creation of value, especially for small and medium enterprises. It is a state of law and it is easy to respect the contracts. In twenty-four hours, one can open a company and have a bank account. It is efficient for transport and logistics and with high-quality personnel. For our business, the legislation is simpler than in China, with no taxes on the import of food products and licenses to import specific products are easy to obtain. Hong Kong is a place where we find a western and Chinese clientele, used to traveling the world and to enjoying high-quality food. This is a trump card that has made it the place in Asia where French, Spanish and Italian food are most appreciated."

One result of this openness is that the market is very competitive. "The city has 5,000 importers of wine, with four or five big importers. Our firm trains specialists in different products. This requires a lot of time and training. What attracts our staff is not the salary so much as the capacity to learn and grow. They should share my passion. My office has no door. I welcome people to walk in," Bossier said. CFF employs Hong Kong people and a limited number of westerners for very technical positions. "I am harder and more demanding on the westerners. I bring them down to earth and teach them to work with Chinese. They must not be arrogant."

He rates Hong Kong as the second city in Asia for high-quality cuisine, after Tokyo. "Japan has the most restaurants in Asia with Michelin star ratings. Hong Kong is second. These two are far ahead of the others, and more sophisticated than Singapore. Hong Kong people like to eat out. The sophistication of Japanese is remarkable. Take patisserie, for example: through their discipline, they have taken it to a higher level, higher than that of French people."

Bossier spends about 60 per cent of the year in Hong Kong. For the rest of the year, he visits countries in Asia where CFF does business and France three or four times a year, to see his mother, aged 89. "I remain very French at heart and take part in activities organized by the French Chamber of Commerce to keep the link." He plans to remain in Hong Kong with his Chinese wife and the apartment they have bought.

What is his advice to Hong Kong people? "Up to now, they have been very open to the world. But the young people now are a little closed . The standard of English is falling, which is disturbing. The parents speak English well, but less so their children. They must seize the opportunity of the Greater Bay Area and not close in, like a village."

He said that Hong Kong remained a very attractive city for Westerners. "Many young people come here to seek opportunities. It is easy to set up a company, easier than Singapore, but costs are very high. If they establish their own firm or find a job with a company here, they can obtain a work visa. Hong Kong remains the main point of entry for investment into China."

Fine Art
Fine Art is one of the strengths of France and its specialists have come here to fulfill their talents. One is Laure Raibaut, who arrived in Hong Kong in 2011 to manage a gallery of contemporary Chinese art. Today she works as an art consultant and university lecturer, with her office in a house she bought on a hilltop in Cheung Chau.

"I am not an expatriate, I am a Hong Konger. The city has allowed me to do things which I could not elsewhere. I would like to stay here for the long term, especially now when we should not leave the ship. I feel a sense of security here." At eight each morning, she walks with her two dogs to a nearby beach for a swim; one joins her in the water, the other plays happily on the beach.

"What I like most about Hong Kong is the kindness of the Chinese people. In Cheung Chau, there are few social barriers. It is a large community; neighbours share with each other, like the cake they have just made. There is no discrimination. I felt this kindness most powerfully in October 2018. On the ferry going home, I had a cardiac attack. I felt intense pain and my heart rate fell to forty per minute (normal is 60-100). I spent the next thirteen days in the emergency room of Chaiwan hospital, a public facility. During that time, I lost fifteen kilograms. My heart rate went up to 168. I was too exhausted to be afraid and I entrusted my life to the care of the medical staff. They put me in a special room with just two beds. The doctors and nurses were so kind, they could not have done more. Several nurses had long shifts, from early morning to late night; they still looked after patients with great attention and kindness. They did all kinds of tests, including MRI, and concluded that it was "burnout", tension of work. For those thirteen days, I paid just HK$1,500. In the room was a Filipina helper with a similar condition. She received the same quality of treatment. When I need to go to hospital, I always go to a public one. Since that experience, I have not traveled to Europe. In New York, I was faced with racism, even towards the French, but never here. Hong Kong Chinese have a gentleness and kindness — unfortunately, most of the expats have a sense of entitlement and superiority, a colonial legacy, I guess."

During her nine years here, Hong Kong has become Asia's largest market for art, with about fifty galleries selling Asian and Western art, modern and classical. With 6,000 pieces, M+ in the West Kowloon Cultural Center will have the biggest collection of Chinese art in the world. "Most of the buyers are rich Mainlanders and overseas Chinese. Hong Kong is most attractive for the galleries because of its low taxes, less than those of New York, Paris or London. The art market is globally unregulated. It is like the Wild West. Anything goes. Hong Kong has also the advantage of being a free port."

Raibaut prefers galleries run by locals. "These owners are very sincere and do real work for artists, nurturing them. They present the artists' best works to the customers. There are good collectors in Hong Kong, who are engaged in art and are not speculators." She is less complimentary about 'imported' galleries run from abroad. "The so-called blue chip galleries, big names from New York, Paris and London, are mostly after the deep pockets of Mainland Chinese. These international galleries have been criticized for bringing second-rate artworks for Art Basel HK, and keeping the top works for the Switzerland or Miami fairs and clients. Rich Mainlanders, and Chinese diaspora collectors see art as a form of investment, more liquid than real estate. They also want to show off that they paid the highest price, notably at auction; it is a question of face. So the market players exploit this."

She said that Hong Kong will preserve this status as Asia's premier art market with two conditions. "One is that the economy goes well. Art pieces are not necessities. The second is that we retain our freedom of expression and creativity. In the Mainland, censorship is quite strictly implemented, and works are taken down, seized, destroyed sometimes. During the era of Deng Xiaoping and Jiang Zemin, there was a degree of liberalization in this area, but not now. That is how the Chinese contemporary art scene could exist and later flourish."

EUROPEANS IN HONG KONG

But, while Hong Kong is a major market, it is not yet a major center of creation, like Paris, New York or London. "The artists here do not have access to adequate studio space, the rents are too expensive. This is a big handicap. Most artists have to teach to make a living and cannot only focus on their work and career. HK artists have been in the shadow of Mainland artists, whose work was heavily bought for speculation. Now they are also in the shadow of Western blue-chip artists whose work is also purchased for speculation. The market focuses on the next best thing or the return. Of course, there are fabulous artists in Hong Kong. Many are quite conceptual, and so the work is not as obvious a commodity as a colorful, grinning self-portrait. HK artists do not 'quote' visually appealing/familiar artworks as much; they often have a sincere message and find very creative ways to translate it through their works. With the reopening of the HK Museum of Art and the long-awaited opening of the M+ and the WKCD (West Kowloon Cultural District), there are hopes for more platforms to recognize HK artists, modern and contemporary. Although the integration of the Palace Museum in the WKCD has sparked debate, there are still institutional and non-profit exhibition opportunities. The government funds are quite focused and often directed to the same artists, but they have the merit of existing," Raibaut said.

Before arriving in Hong Kong, Raibaut had a diverse career in the art world. She graduated in 2001 with a Bachelor of Law and Economy in Science-Po Bordeaux, followed by a Master of Art History in 2003 from Bordeaux III. In 2004, she obtained a Master of Art and Archeology from the School of Oriental and African Studies in London. There she also studied Japanese and Chinese art history and archeology. She holds a Master of Chinese Art and Archeology from the Sorbonne. She worked as a researcher and curator at museums and institutions in France and China, including the Musee d'Orsay in Paris. She also studied at the Central Academy of Fine Arts in Beijing and worked for Platform China Art Institute in Beijing. She lived in Beijing for two years and learned Mandarin. It was an opportunity to know about modern Chinese art and meet the artists who created it, such as Zhang Xiaogang (張曉剛), Zeng Fanzhi (曾梵志), Yue Minjun (岳敏君), Sui Jianguo (隋建國) and Jia Aili (賈藹力).

In 2007, she moved to New York, to work for the Chinese Contemporary Gallery and Eli Klein Fine Art. "When I was working there, friends moved to Hong Kong and told me that it was the future capital of art in the world. Then Nicole Schoeni proposed to meet me if I flew from New York to Seattle Airport. She hired me to run the Schoeni Art Gallery in Hong Kong, with the project of an artist-in-residence program and school and foundation for artists. It had opened in Hong Kong in 1992 to sell contemporary Chinese art. It seemed like a fabulous opportunity, so I took it."

The biggest change was the pace of work. "As they say, a second in Hong Kong is a minute in New York. That is very accurate. Work in New York is intense, but not like here. You have only time for work and not for a life outside." Language was not a problem; she mainly used English and Mandarin. She does not speak Cantonese. From her two years in Beijing, she gained a good knowledge of Chinese artists, some of whom she knew personally. "I wanted to find new talent and rising stars. I knew little of Hong Kong artists, who had been left in the shadows by the artists of China. I was fascinated by the works of Samson Young (楊嘉輝) and Hung Keung (洪強).It was hard to make people appreciate their work and impossible to sell them. They are well known now, but not then. They are very conceptual, working with music, software and motion sensors. To bring a better awareness of them and show the work the gallery had since its inception in discovering rising talents, we produced short documentaries, with interviews. They were available on YouTube and documented the Mainland superstars that Nicole's father worked with, alongside the younger emerging artists from the Mainland and HK." In 2012, she organized the exhibition to celebrate the twentieth anniversary of the Schoeni Gallery.

During her first year in Hong Kong, Raibaut lived in a small apartment in the Mid-Levels near the Mosque. Then she moved to Cheung Chau, with a better living environment for a family. She rented an apartment; the owner announced that he wanted to take it back. "I spent six months looking for a place to live. It was impossible to find anything to rent. Each Saturday, I took a six-year-old French boy, the son of my closest friend and who spoke Cantonese, around the island in the search. He found this house at the top of a hill, twelve minutes' walk from the ferry terminal. The price was HK$2.3 million. I could not obtain a loan in Hong Kong, but my family in France helped me to get one. It will be paid off just before 2047. I have the two upper floors, with two bedrooms. One of them is my office now." So Raibaut avoided the grievous mistake of many expatriates who do not buy a property of their own. If they lose their job or regular income, they face homelessness.

Her next two jobs were at auction houses Bonhams and Christie's. "It was very intense and very competitive. We were competing not only against the other auction houses but against each other. We hid our clients and our artworks from each other. Another challenge was to be the lone Westerner in an office of Chinese. At Bonham's, my colleagues invited me to lunch and spoke mostly Cantonese together; I did not understand it, but at least they invited me. At Christie's, the boss was Taiwanese, so we spoke Mandarin. There my colleagues spoke English but at best ignored me; at worst, they really tried to ruin all my efforts."

She and her colleagues worked a twelve-hour day, often into the early morning of the next day, as well as weekends.

In 2016, she started to work with the Hong Kong Arts Center. "It was a very good adventure for me. It was the first institution I worked with that was non-profit. I had a good relationship with (Executive Director) Connie Lam. I organized an exhibition *Mekong New Mythologies – Enfants du Mekong*, to support the charity Enfants du Mekong. So we thought to focus on the liquid element of geography to bring together artists whose works were sold to benefit the charity." She was head of Visual Arts for Le French May and Lumieres, two festivals initiated by the Association Culturelle France – Hong Kong. For Le French May, she produced the exhibitions *School of Nice* (2018) and *Niki de Saint-Phalle* (2019). She is a lecturer for the BA and MA programs at the Hong Kong Polytechnic University.

From 2014 to 2016, she has been on the board of the Friends of the Art Museum of the Chinese University of Hong Kong. She recently curated their thirty-fifth anniversary show at the Rotunda in Exchange Square, titled *Nurturing Creativity*. She is currently working as a consultant, based at home. "I have enough projects. People contact me. Previously, I used to go back to France once a year, but not since the cardiac attack. I loved to savor the markets of my youth, in my home town of Nice. I miss that. I continue to provide financial support to my mother."

The French community here has strong links with members of the Hong Kong. They have come through L'Alliance Francaise (法國文化協會), France's many cultural activities and a prominent business profile. Presidents of L'Alliance Française have included Lord Kadoorie, Dr Hans Tang, Judge Henry Litton and Judge Roberto Ribeiro. The French government has awarded the Légion d'Honneur (法國榮譽軍團勳章), its highest civilian decoration, to several of its closest partners in Hong

Kong. They include Lord Kadoorie and three members of his family—Sir Elly, Sir Horace and Sir Michael—as well as Sir Wayne Leung (梁偉賢), Dr James Kung (孔祥勉) and Sir David Li (李國寶). In 2002, the members here formed the Hong Kong chapter of the Club of La Légion d'Honneur. Since 2006, it has provided nearly 1,000 scholarships to students from Hong Kong and Macao to study in France to perfect their knowledge of the language and discover French culture. It has also organized a series of distinguished lectures by Professor Philippe Ciarlet (菲立普·希阿雷教授) of City University with French Nobel Prize winners. In June 2020, the club donated 30,000 surgical masks to the French International School.

Dr James Kung was the driving force behind the most important scientific co-operation between Hong Kong and France—the Hong Kong University-Pasteur Research Pole (PRP -香港大學巴斯德研究中心), established in November 1999, to study infectious diseases. The French partner is the Pasteur Institute of Paris (法國巴斯德研究院), one of the most famous medical science centers in the world. It was the first branch of the Pasteur Institute to be set up overseas after World War II. Following the SARS outbreak, which profoundly changed the perception of the risk from infectious diseases, HKU PRP has focused on host-pathogen interactions with particular emphasis on respiratory viruses and other viruses that represent a public health threat for Hong Kong and the region. For fourteen years until his retirement in July 2020, its co-director was Sri Lankan virologist Professor Malik Peiris, an internationally famous specialist in infectious diseases. He conducted crucial scientific research, notably on the creation of a diagnostic test for SARS in 2003, and studies on H5N1 mutating virus strains and conditions which enable avian influenza transmissions. In 2017, he was promoted to the rank of Officer of the Légion d'Honneur.

Paul Clerc-Renaud, a member of the Légion d'Honneur Club, recalled, "I had a great admiration for Dr Kung and, when he asked me to join the board of the Pasteur HK University Research Center, which he also chaired and very generously endowed, I accepted gladly. For the next ten years, which included the SARS crisis, I followed closely the wonderful work of the Center with Professor Ralf Altmeyer and Roberto Bruzzone, its successive CEOs, and Prof Malik Peiris, its chief scientific officer. We organized several fund-raising events including a gala dinner with French actress Sophie Marceau. I was glad to accompany [former] Chief Executive Carrie Lam on her official visit to Paris in June 2018 during which a convention was signed between Pasteur and HK to found a new ambitious research center at HK Science Park." In addition, there are more than 160 partnerships between French and Hong Kong universities, which allow students to obtain diplomas in both places.

Pillar of the Community
Paul Clerc-Renaud has been a pillar of the French community in Hong Kong for more than forty years. In 1977, he arrived at Kai Tak airport on Chung Yeung Festival (重陽節). Central was a giant construction site for the first MTR line and the French consulate had just 1,000 of its citizens registered. He did not expect to live in the city so long. Ever since, he has been a front-line participant in the business and diplomatic life of the SAR and of China.

"Reflecting on the last forty-three years I spent in Hong Kong, I am grateful for all the opportunities this extraordinary city has offered me," he said. "Despite the toll it sometimes took on my family life due to constant traveling and long hours and all the crises and upheavals we went through, its spirit of resilience has always inspired me and my colleagues. I treasure the friendship of so many Hong Kong and French persons I had the opportunity to know and work with. I just hope that, as Hong Kong moves into a new phase of its history and I move to a less active and more reflective phase of my life, this proverbial resilience will again show itself."

Clerc-Renaud was born in Lyon in 1947. His father was a textile engineer following in the family silk industry tradition; this explains the city's early links with China—HSBC's first European establishment was in Lyon. He was educated at Lycée Ampère in Lyon and then at France's top business school: Ecole des Hautes Etudes Commerciales (HEC) where he studied International Trade and Finance. After graduation in 1970 and two round-the-world trips, he joined SACA, one of France's largest trading companies. It sent him to New Zealand to open its office there; he stayed for several years, before moving to Australia where he started a chain of bakeries in partnership with SACA. Then the company invited him to Hong Kong, to audit and reorganize two subsidiaries it had started in the 1960s.

"I stayed with my wife and twin toddlers at the Mandarin for a brief period," he recalled. "Central was a gigantic construction site where the first MTR line was under construction in open trenches. Most were built by the French company Dragages, which had also built Kai Tak Airport. It was impossible to walk in Central with a double buggy—my son had taken a liking for cracking the glass on the ground with his teeth So we quickly found a flat in Baguio Villa with a full view of Telegraph Bay from our balcony. Over the years, we have lived in Tai Tam, the Peak, Mid-Levels and finally Sheung Wan. In 1977, the rent for a three-bedroom flat was HK$5,000 and for a villa HK$20,000. They already seemed expensive."

In 1977, the French community in Hong Kong was small—1,000 persons registered at the consulate, half of them recent arrivals from Vietnam and Cambodia. The leading French firms were two shipping companies Messageries Maritime and Chargeurs; their freighters stayed in midstream long enough for the captains to entertain their French clients royally for lunch on board, including camembert and saucissons. The other French firms were banks, construction companies and a few specialized trading firms, handling silk and import of wine, food and electronic components. The consulate was in the Hang Seng building and the residence of the Consul General in a colonial mansion on Old Peak Road. In 1981, he would exchange it for a residence on the Peak, two floors in Admiralty and a few flats plus a sum which helped to build a new French school in Jardines Lookout; in 1977, it was in an old British military hospital on Bowen Road, opposite Island School. Alliance Française was already active and French comedy films were popular. They were distributed commercially by Pathé Overseas, one of the two companies Clerc-Renaud was to audit. His other mission was to streamline and reorganize SACA Far East, a trading company.

"After the sedate pace of business in New Zealand and Australia, my first impression of Hong Kong was overwhelming," Clerc-Renaud said. My office was in Connaught Road opposite the car ferry. I could observe the constant flow of cars and trucks climbing the ramps to cross the harbor to Jordan. The business world was even more hectic. It was dominated by the British hongs—Jardines, Swire, Hutchison and HSBC. But, below the surface, a whole world of small Hong Kong traders and factory owners was frantically betting on the first signs of China opening. The former gathered for lunch at the beautiful old Hong Kong Club; the latter did their business in the many dim sum places and dai pai dongs on the island and in Kowloon. I had to learn fast and got private tutors to teach me the basics in Cantonese and Mandarin. In the evening, the favorite spots

EUROPEANS IN HONG KONG

to entertain visitors were the Macao ferry car park night market, the sampans of the Causeway Bay typhoon shelter or the tour on Aberdeen harbor, which inevitably ended up at the Jumbo floating restaurant. Weekend junk outings always ended at the seafood restaurants on Lamma, Po Toi or Lei Yu Moon."

After six months of auditing work, Clerc-Renaud decided to sell his shares in Australia and accept the offer to settle down in Hong Kong and manage the two companies. He enjoyed the film distribution work as they had their own projection room and welcomed all the French film stars—but it was not profitable, so they sold it. He picked an excellent time to settle in Hong Kong—the door into China was slowly opening and would provide abundant opportunities for his company in the future. SACA had a diversified business—it represented French engineering firms, like Technip and Geostock, and bought goods for French firms. This sourcing business was taking off with the arrival of French hypermarket chains for which it bought textiles and toys in Hong Kong and Macao, electronics in Hong Kong and Korea and hardware in Taiwan and then China. At the time factory buildings were buzzing all over Kwun Tong, Lai Chi Kok, Kwai Chung and Wong Chuk Hang, and their concentration made sourcing easy and competition fierce. That's where the Darwinian process produced some of Hong Kong's wealthier families. But China was beckoning, and Clerc-Renaud began a forty-year relationship with the Mainland. He started by attending the Canton Trade Fair twice a year; at that time, it was the only venue available for foreign companies to do business with Chinese firms.

"My first fair in the autumn of 1977 was still in full Maoist style, with huge portraits of Mao and successor Hua Guofeng (華國鋒) and posters saying, "With you [Hua] in charge, my heart is at ease" (你辦事，我放心—what Mao is said to have told

Hua. I would not miss the fairs for the next twenty years, for fear of losing the right to the most coveted invitation. Initially, the Dongfang Hotel (東方宾館) was overwhelmed and the accommodation very basic—sometimes just a table in a common room. My first visit to Beijing was on May 1, 1978, invited by a diplomat friend. The crowds on Tiananmen Square were huge, mostly provincial visitors who looked at us foreigners with amazement."

Clerc-Renaud spent much effort promoting the French company Geostock; it was the world leader for underground storage of oil and gas. That would be the ideal way to remove giant storage tanks on Ap Lei Chao and Tsing Yi and make space for development. The company's geological surveys showed that the granite would be ideal for cavern storage. The oil companies and developers were interested. But the red tape of the Hong Kong Government for such a new technology was too slow—and other solutions were preferred. China's Ministry of Mining was also interested and invited Clerc-Renaud to Beijing to study the possibility of building underground caverns in Shaanxi in exchange for its coal. "However we realized that we would also have to build a railway to bring the coal to the port!"

In 1980, with some of SACA's shareholders, Clerc-Renaud co-founded Fargo Services; it would become the holding company of the group as it continued to diversify and expand into China. In 1984, it opened its first Mainland office, a room in the White Swan Hotel in Guangzhou; others followed in Beijing, Kunming and other provincial capitals. The company later bought its own office space in Shanghai overlooking the golden roofs of Jing'an temple.

In 1985, the firm was forced to restructure because of the appreciation of the US dollar against the French franc, to US$1-10 FF. Clerc-Renaud was helped by a French businessman, Bertrand

EUROPEANS IN HONG KONG

Jalon, who has been his partner in the holding company ever since. "We developed the sale of French equipment to China, first with buyback of the end-product made by our machines: woodworking machines, tobacco and paper machinery and printing equipment. Then we added equipment for the aluminum and packaging industries that China needed."

The period after the military crackdown on student-led protest in Beijing in June 1989 was difficult. "Hong Kong had a crisis of confidence and the brain drain affected many of the leading middle management of foreign companies. We decided to diversify geographically and opened an office in Ho Chi Minh City in Vietnam, which was starting the reform of its economy, to promote French equipment: cable cars, tunneling machines, construction materials and industrial machinery," he said.

In 1993, as part of its diversification, Fargo created Far East Lockers, a chain of electronic luggage lockers. Its first installation was opened on May 2, 1994, at the Canton Road ferry terminal by K.Y. Yeung, then Secretary for Transport. The company continued to open offices in China, Thailand, India and South Africa as its business grew and diversified into distribution of chemicals and foodstuffs. Its telecom operations broadened from sourcing into distribution of wireless communications components and then its own products. In 1998, Fargo started opening stores in China — first in Beijing, then tier-one cities — to distribute Jacadi children's wear, French brands of ladies' underwear, and furniture which became a big part of the business. It also opened stores for famous French brands Ligne Roset and Hugues Chevalier; but their price limited the sales to China's main cities. In 2007, it launched its own furniture brand HC28, designed in France, manufactured in its own factory in Beijing and sold exclusively in its stores in China and abroad.

In addition to running Fargo, Clerc-Renaud found the time to represent his country. In 1985, he was appointed Conseiller du Commerce Extérieur de la France (CCE), (French Foreign Trade Adviser) and later chaired the CCE Hong Kong chapter for two years. In 1986, he was one of the founders and early presidents of the French Business Association (FBA) in Hong Kong, which later became the French Chamber of Commerce. In October 1992, with the French Trade Commission and other partners, the FBA organized a major event, the Chinese World symposium in Hong Kong. They brought 350 French business leaders and the French Foreign Trade Minister for a two-day forum. Then they took half of them in buses to discover the new Shenzhen and Zhuhai SEZs and then Nansha, Foshan and Guangzhou.

"Everyone was taken aback by the speed and scope of the construction day and night in the Pearl River Delta (PRD).. To avoid the enormous traffic jams of container trucks, Gordon Wu and Henry Fok opened for us the HK-Guangzhou motorway still under construction and we entered Guangzhou with a police escort. That was for many French companies the start of a fascination with the potential of China. We subsequently held three equally successful Chinese World symposiums in HK — in 1997, 2003 after SARS and in 2007." The late 1990s were a good period for Hong Kong, with confidence returning. The French Chamber developed quickly with the growth of the French community. The year 1997 was full of excitement with the handover. We partied under the rain all night at the Regent, and I joined the official banquet the next day offered by Lu Ping to the business community." Lu was director of the Hong Kong and Macau Affairs Office (HKMAO). He retired shortly after the handover.

In his role as leader of the FBA and as Chairman of the Europe committee of the Hong Kong General Chamber, Clerc-Renaud led or joined many delegations to Beijing to meet ministers of the Chinese government; he also hosted delegations of the French government to China and Hong Kong. The Hong Kong government appointed him as a member of the Hong Kong-France Business Council; it worked to improve economic relations between the two sides. He joined missions every two years of Hong Kong companies to France and various HK promotion roadshows to Europe.

"I had the chance of getting to know some remarkable Hong Kong personalities. Dr James Kung, under whom I served as director of both the Legion d'Honneur HK Chapter and of the Pasteur HK University Research Center, was my mentor and a very generous Confucian gentleman. When he passed away, the Hon Sir David Li took over the chair of the Legion d'Honneur chapter and I much admired him both as a great financier and a very generous leader of the community. I also had the honor of working with Dr Stanley Ho who recently passed away and [the late] Alan Li (at that time chairman of the Jockey Club) to find an iconic building that could house a French Club. They taught me a lot about the culture and ethics of the Hong Kong business world, in matters of trust (xinyong), courtesy, risk-taking and community service. I was also inspired by the Hon Justice Roberto Ribeiro who chaired Alliance Française for many years and became a close friend. I also enjoyed my contacts with Hong Kong students both those of the European program of Baptist University, on whose advisory board I served at its creation, and students from all other universities to whom our Legion d'Honneur chapter awarded 100 annual scholarships for study trips to France. Their profiles, motivations and worries varied along the years but their love of study, of Hong Kong and of the French language always impressed me."

In 2013, the National Committee of the Conseil du Commerce Exterieur (Council for Foreign Trade) of which he was a director launched a vast survey titled "La Chine Hors Les Murs" (China Outside the Walls) to obtain feedback from the 150 CCE committees all over the world about China's activities in their respective countries. The committee drew up a report and decided to set up a permanent observatory of "La Chine Hors Les Murs" and publish a newsletter, now bimonthly; Clerc-Renaud has been a co-director and co-editor ever since.

With the consulate and several academics, he also co-authored a book on the history of the French presence in Hong Kong. It was published in October 2013. The title is *Hong Kong – French Connections, from the 19th Century to the Present Day*. The book was launched at Victoria House, the residence of the Chief Secretary for Administration.

In 2013, Clerc-Renaud turned 66. Because of age, he and his partner Bertrand Jalon decided to gradually divest themselves of their business ventures, preferably through managed or leveraged buyouts, over the next seven years. "Those years were marked by some successes in Vietnam (equipment) and China (furniture), but also difficulties resulting from the 2008 financial crisis for our telecom ventures; they were absorbed by a HK-listed company together with their French management. In Hong Kong, after several years promoting our partners SURYS—a world leader in the security features of official documents—we were rewarded with the contract for the security features of the new HK identity card, which is ongoing."

Now Clerc-Renaud divides his time between Hong Kong and Europe. He spends about four months a year in the South of France, where he has a house, and eight months in Hong Kong, Vietnam and Bali, where one of his children lives. The others are spread between Canada, the UK and Germany. Each pursued their own path and none of them decided to follow in his steps in the HK business world.

EUROPEANS IN HONG KONG

On March 14, 2016, the Consul General and French companies announced the launch of French Tech Hong Kong (「香港法國科技中心」). It aims to create a French tech community here and in Shenzhen, facilitate the access of French talent to the city and support them and develop innovation. It was the fifth such French Tech hub, after New York, San Francisco, Tokyo and Israel. As of 2014, thirty-four subsidiaries of French companies in the ICT sector had set up in Hong Kong, generating €260 million of profits and providing 900 jobs. One of them, 8 Securities, which provides mobile trading and investing services in Asia, has raised US$17 million since its creation in 2010. French Tech helps French people create start-ups in Hong Kong, with advice and mentors, help with financing, networks and hiring staff.

Vivian Meriguet, co-founder of Wild at Heart, said that there were fifty companies involved in French Tech, ranging from small start-ups to firms with 200 people; they are in sectors ranging from law and finance to new technologies and green tech. "French firms choose Hong Kong for financial and technological reasons, but do their production on the other side of the border," he said. "Beijing wants to integrate the whole zone into a Silicon Valley of Asia, while keeping Hong Kong as a financial center. Our aim is to advance French knowhow and also to attract Chinese investors to France. We want to run workshops and conferences for the French firms and create close links with investors, firms and local students."

One success story is that of Karen Contet Farzam, who in 2014 established WHub, Hong Kong's largest start-up community with over 3,000 listed on its website. She spent most of her childhood in Japan before going back to France for higher education. She has a double degree engineering diploma and a Master of International Finance from HEC business school in Paris. She returned to Japan to work as an Exotic Equity Derivatives trader in JP Morgan in Tokyo, before landing in Hong Kong in 2010. In 2014, she decided with a friend to set up WHub. "We were both fascinated by the enthusiasm entrepreneurs have for what they do and we felt there needed to be a platform for them to showcase not only their product, but their passion." She took a three-month course in coding. Now WHub has its headquarters in Hong Kong wit staff in London, Israel and India and a network of more than 500 partners worldwide. In September 2019, the company raised US$3 million in a funding round.

"Hong Kong has seen extensive activity in its start-up economic system with an estimate of more than 3,000 start-ups," she said. "It is uniquely positioned to allow fast and high scalability. Products can be tested quickly due to its hyper-connected population. Its small market forces start-ups to think globally from Day One. There is a strong sense of genuine support and solidarity within the ecosystem …The city now boasts of nine home-grown unicorns, including four FinTech unicorns … WHub's Passion is to boost start-ups, foster the growth of the start-up ecosystem and bring Hong Kong/GBA (Greater Bay Area) to the top on the global map of Start-up Ecosystems."

Learning French

One of the best known symbols of France in Hong Kong is l'Alliance Francaise (AF). It was founded in 1953 as a non-profit association for the promotion of French language and culture. Today it has three centers, in Wanchai, Jordan and Shatin. It has eighty-five employees, including twenty-five to twenty-six in the administration and sixty teachers giving courses to more than 6,000 students, adults and young people, each year. It is one of the largest language institutions for French in Asia. Its sixty qualified native French-speaking teachers offer specialized courses, private tuition, workshops, immersion days, outings to museums, French dining and other experiences. Each year it organizes major cultural events, such as the French Film Festival in November and the Make Music Festival in June. It also takes part in numerous programs of Le French May, which it has helped to launch and develop since 1993. It has a multimedia library with more than 9,000 French books, CDs and DVDs.

Its first president was Pierre Huret and its first offices were on the second floor of Saint Louis Mansion on 20 MacDonnell Road in Mid-Levels It offered a reading room, meeting room, office and a large library, which by 1958, had 6,600 books and thirty French magazines and newspapers. During the 1960s, it had 3,000 students a year. It moved many times before buying offices in Hennessy Road, Wanchai in 1971 and Jordan Road, Kowloon in 1975. The number of students increased to 5,000 a year and the AF launched an annual French Film Festival. AF has been listed as Charity Organization since 1979.

It was both a center for activities for the French community and also a meeting place for Francophone and Francophile Chinese. They included former students of the French-speaking Aurora University in Shanghai, who fled to Hong Kong after 1949. In education, it offered French classes and conferences, as well as local radio programs. It hosted music events, debates on writers' texts, exhibitions, and film screenings.

"From its foundation in 1883 under a committee led by Jules Verne, the idea was to set up local organizations with local people to promote the language and culture," said Jean-Sebastian Attié, the director general. "At that time, the resources of the State were quite limited. Therefore, the branches of AF developed on local goodwill and the work of local people. Following World War II, the French State started to provide more support and be more active, in terms of means and teachers. This led to a tremendous development. However, its share of the budget of AF has always been relatively limited. In 2014, for example, the global budget of AFs in the world was €220 million euros, and French State global spending for AFs was about €40 million."

The AF in Hong Kong was fortunate to have as its President for twelve years Lord Kadoorie, one of the most prominent businessmen in the city. "He and his wife Muriel were fluent in French. They were Francophiles. Lord Kadoorie also served as President of Honor and was on the Board of Directors. We had the benefits of his time, ideas and connections," said Attié. Lord Kadoorie initiated the purchase of the AF center in Kowloon and supported the association for more than twenty years. The next president was Dr Hans Tang (湯于翰), one of Hong Kong's leading physicians, from 1980 to 1984; the Honorable Justice Henry Litton (烈顯倫)from 1985 to 2000; and, from 2000 to 2016, the Honorable Justice Roberto Ribeiro (李義), who was made a Legion d'Honneur by the French state. AF then appointed in 2016 Mr Edouard Ettedgui, a prominent personality in Hong Kong business. The engagement of such eminent figures with their connections and experience has been essential for an institution that needs financial support from individuals, companies and foundations to run its wide diversity of programs. "AF bought the Wanchai and Kowloon sites with loans and its own money," said Attié. "Our board manages our institution fantastically well. But today it would be almost impossible to buy the two sites. We also had a building in North Point, which we had to sell in 1995."

In the 1960s, the AF established the first language laboratories in the city and broadcast audiovisual courses on the radio and television in 1965. The number of students rose from sixty-six in 1953 to 4,700 in 1970 and 10,000 in 1980. Its professors included Pierre Rickmans—better known as Simon Leys, a famous Sinologist—and his Royal Highness Henrik, Prince Consort of Denmark. After the military crackdown in Beijing in June 1989, the AF in Hong Kong became the largest in the world in terms of numbers, with six centers and 12,000 students enrolled each year. The largest number of registrations was 45,000 in 1991, when the AF was operating out of seven locations. It was a world record for students of the Alliance in one city. Canada was one of the favorite countries for emigration by Hong Kong people; knowledge of French, one of the country's two official languages, greatly helps an application, especially to the French-speaking Province of Quebec.

The annual budget of AF in Hong Kong is about HK$40 million. "The courses pay for themselves," said Attié. "Cultural events usually cost more than they bring in. We raise money from sales of tickets to concerts and other events but it is not enough. We do not own a cinema or any cultural space. We need to rely on sponsors and partners." This is not a simple task. Hong Kong is a vibrant city with many cultural, artistic and sporting events; they are also, like AF, looking for sponsors and financial support, as are non-governmental organizations. AF has a team dedicated to this task. "Sponsors enjoy big and visible events, like Le French May or The French Film Festival. It is more difficult to finance one-off events, like an individual concert or play. There is also the competition from many other events and an increasing trend to fund Asian cultures. French culture is also present in Hong Kong, in bakeries, restaurants and shops. It is more widely accessible than ever."

Teaching French is the core mission of the AF. It is no simple matter persuading Hong Kong people to devote time and energy to study a second foreign language; it is full of irregular verbs, forms that change with past, present and future and nouns that are masculine or feminine — often for no apparent reason. Young people in Hong Kong have a heavy study and examination load that aims to make them fluent in written and spoken Mandarin and English as well as their native Cantonese. The AF has addressed this problem by offering fancy dress balls, dancing, music, conferences, festivals, fashion and excursions and picnics on cruise ships. Attending AF events, therefore, is fun, chic and good for networking—not only about improving your vocabulary and pronunciation.

The Alliance organizes musical concerts, dance and theater performances and lectures by prominent scholars, in many premises in Hong Kong. In May 1970, Marceau, one of the world's most famous mimes, gave two performances at City Hall. In 1973, the AF opened a gallery in its premises on Gloucester Road, to promote French and Hong Kong artists. It was managed by a young American Francophone, Sandra Walters; she exhibited lithographs from the Ecole de Paris for the first time in Hong Kong. In 1993, AF established with the Consulate General of France, Le French May, and ran it for about ten years. Since then, the festival has developed as an independent charity. Students and friends of AF wrote Le *Journal de Hong Kong*, which was first published on December 1, 1970, and ran for eleven years when it was replaced by the magazine *Paroles*. It was the city's first monthly magazine in French and Chinese.

"Of our adult students, 10-15 percent are learning for professional reasons, to prepare to emigrate or to rise in their firm," said Attié. "They can take intensive classes, up to twelve hours a week, or have private lessons. For the others, the main objective is leisure and to have an intake of oxygen in their busy day and rhythm. Hong Kong people enjoy learning new things and are very curious. A class is three hours of enjoyment," he said.

"For the children, the teachers provide a combination of learning and playing in French, with songs, toys and games. The children love it. Our teachers are very creative. The parents are also looking for academic gain, such as entry to international schools or education in the UK and Canada. The teachers find a balance to this regards," he said.

The AF was created in Paris on July 21, 1883, by a group of people, including scientist Louis Pasteur, diplomat Ferdinand de Lesseps and writers Jules Verne and Ernest Renan, to promote the French language and culture in the world. It has a location in Paris, sites throughout France for foreign students and 850 locations in 135 countries in five continents. It teaches nearly 500,000 students a year around the world, with over six million taking part in its cultural activities. Its business model is different from that of the Goethe Institut, the Instituto Cervantes and the British Council, which are part of their respective governments. The AFs are independent franchises run by a local committee and a President. The French government provides an average of ten per cent of its budget; the rest comes mainly from fees from its courses, but also from exams and cultural activities.

Attié said that 100 million people in the world were native speakers of French, with 120 million learning it as a second language. "That ranks it second after English as a language of study, ahead of Spanish and German. The study of French is still growing in Europe, Africa, the Middle East, Latin America and some parts in Asia like Indonesia, Malaysia, or China."

French Bookshop
For those seeking books, magazines and other material in French, there is only one place to go—a room on the second floor of an office building in the heart of Central is home to the only French-language bookshop in China—Parentheses, established in 1989 by Madeline Progin, a Swiss. The space of 100 square meters offers more than 20,000 titles, including new books, classics, children's books, novels, tour guides, comics, dozens of weekly

and monthly magazines, specialized publications on China and Asia, language-learning material and DVDs. Progin earned not a dollar for the first six years but is proud to have sustained it for more than thirty years. "It is to share my passion for reading—sometimes this passion is too strong!" she said.

Progin arrived in Hong Kong in 1979, following her husband, who had moved to the city in 1976, as the Asian representative of a Swiss watch group. At the end of 1987, a Belgian entrepreneur opened a shop on the fourth floor of a building in Duke of Wellington Street in Central. "He ran a small food shop and was a headhunter, in addition to offering all kinds of services; he also had a few books. I immediately became a good client," she said. In 1989, the Belgian put the business up for sale. "I wanted to take up a professional activity again and it was an ideal opportunity to do so," she said. Her husband gave her the capital, with the condition that she not put one centime more into the bookshop. She followed his advice but earned nothing for the first six years.

"It took time to build up a stock of books, organize orders and establish a turnover. During the era of fax and before computers, it was sometimes difficult to communicate with France." In 2001, she moved to a larger space, 100 square meters, on the second floor of the same building. Its market extends far beyond Hong Kong, with clients coming from Shenzhen and Guangzhou. "We are well known abroad. For a long time, we were the only ones in Asia." It buys from the major publishing houses of France, including Hachette, R. Laffont, Le Seuil, Actes Sud, Gallimard, Flammarion and others. It also has everything needed for those who want to learn French, from the primary to the advanced level.

With the larger space, Progin began to organize meetings and speeches by visiting authors and cartoonists. She held a book-signing event with an author each month. They have included

EUROPEANS IN HONG KONG

Jean Giraud, also known as Mobius, Pierre Gagnaire, Michel Houellebecq, Philippe Franck, Berberian, Pierrette Fleutiaux, actress Juliette Binoche, and Gao Xingjian (高行健), one of only two Chinese to win the Nobel Prize for Literature. Born in 1940, Gao studied French at Beijing Foreign Studies University and, during the Cultural Revolution, was sent to hard labor in Anhui Province for six years, like tens of thousands of other intellectuals. He had to burn much of what he wrote in the countryside, for fear of being denounced as a dissident. During the 1980s, he began to write extensively, with one of his best known works *Soul Mountain* (靈山). It was first published in Chinese in Taipei in 1990 and in French in 1995. In the late 1980s, Gao moved to Bagnolet, near Paris. A political drama, *Fugitives*, refers to the Tiananmen protests of 1989; this resulted in all his works being banned from performance in China. He became a French citizen in 1998. He received the Nobel Prize for Literature in 2000. After the announcement, the Beijing government said he was not Chinese, but French. Mo Yan (莫言) won the prize in 2012 — Beijing considers him a Chinese.

The bookshop's clients include members of the public, schools, universities, public institutions, consulates and embassies in Hong Kong and in neighboring countries. Among those in Hong Kong, half are French-speaking local people and the other half expatriates.

In honor of Progin's work to promote the language and literature, the French government awarded her the Order of Arts and Letters in 2004 and the National Order of Merit in 2012.

Progin was born in Lignieres, in Neuchatel, a French-speaking canton of Switzerland. Her father was a farmer. It was from an aunt that she acquired a love of reading. After moving to Hong Kong, she taught biology for one year at the French International School. At the end of each visit to Europe, her suitcases were loaded with books. The critical moment came in late 1989, when the opportunity came to start her own venture. She spent her own money to buy the books and redecorate the space to turn it into a proper bookshop. It was a financial risk. The Francophone community in Hong Kong numbered only several thousand; interest among local people was mainly from students of French or those who had returned after studying in a French-speaking country. The market was limited.

How have you continued for so many years? "Certainly not for money. Some have the impression that the books are expensive. But I must pay my rent, the shipment of the books and my employees. If I retain this shop, it is above all my passion for books, too strong perhaps. For example, I love to work on Saturdays, when people are less stressed and have more time to spend in the bookshop. It is almost a library more than a bookshop."

Born in 1945, her husband Mark is also Swiss, a native of Peseux. As a young man, he was a watchmaker. Then a Swiss watch group invited him to be its representative in Asia, based in Hong Kong. At the end of 1981, he opened his own business. He gave it up in 2007. He has traveled widely in Mongolia, including a journey of 3,500 kilometers by bicycle across the Gobi in 2016.

(Note — https://hongkong.consulfrance.org/Bestowal-ceremony-on-the-Legion-of

Please see this website for image of Madame Progin receiving her Order of Merit at the French Consulate-General in 2012)

French International School

For parents who wanted their children to be educated in the French language, the best choice is the French International School (FIS) with history of sixty years. Today it has more than 2,700 pupils between four and eighteen, on four different campuses.

EUROPEANS IN HONG KONG

They represent forty nationalities. It has two streams—one in French and one in English—and aims to produce students fluent in both languages. Half the graduates go to study in France, the other half study in Canada, the United States and Britain.

The school opened in 1963. Its aim was to cater for French children who were in the city for a limited period and wanted to follow the same curriculum of schools in their mother country. Hong Kong had schools managed by religious orders, with many priests and nuns from France; but they taught most classes in English and offered French only as an option. None followed the curriculum of the French Ministry of Education in the mother language. The two founders of the school were Suzanne Hiltermann and Iny Houel, both of Dutch origin. Hiltermann was the wife of Baron Van Aerssen, Consul General of the Netherlands. During World War II, she was active in the Resistance, a member of the 'Dutch-Paris network' that sheltered more than 120 Allied pilots who were shot down and helped them escape from France. The Gestapo arrested her on February 27, 1944; after several brutal interrogations, it sent her to the Ravensbruck concentration camp on April 18, 1944. She was liberated on April 23, 1945. In 1946, US President Harry S. Truman awarded her the Medal of Freedom for her work during the war. Houel was the director of the Alliance Francaise and wife of the military attaché at the French Consulate. The two women drew up a project for a middle school and lycee with the Center National de Tele-Enseignement in Vanves, a forerunner of the Center National d'Enseignement (The National Center for Long-Distance Teaching).

The first students attended classes only in the mornings, in the premises of the Alliance Francaise. Many were children of technicians and engineers who came to build the Shek Pik Dam. In 1964, the thirty-five students moved to Bethanie in

Pokfulam, formerly the sanatorium of the MEP. The number of students increased from seventy in 1969 to 150 in 1975. They used several premises, including a former military hospital in Borrett Road. Then the Hong Kong government gave official approval to the school. In exchange, it would open twenty-five per cent of the student body to international students and teach them in English; the school would have two streams. The French International School was officially born in 1984, in a new building in the Jardine's Lookout district; it had 540 students, of whom 150 were in the international stream. In 1988, it became the first international school in Hong Kong to receive the authorization to become an International Baccalaureate (IB) World School. By 1995, the number of students had reached 1,000.

On July 1, 1997, work began on a new school in Bluepool Road. In 1999, the middle school and FIS moved there. By 2010, the number of students reached 2,000, making it the largest French school in the Asia-Pacific region. The school continued to use the facilities at Jardine's Lookout. In 2011, part of the primary school students moved to a new site in Chaiwan, a former Catholic school built in 1952. The fourth site opened at Tseung Kwan O in September 2018. By 2020, the number of students reached more than 2,700. There are two streams, one following the French national curriculum and leading to the Baccalaureat Francais; the other follows the British curriculum leading to the General Certificate of Secondary Education (GCSE) and the IB.

In the 2017/2018 school year, David Tran became the Principal. From 2013 to 2017, he served as Principal of the Lycee Pasteur of Sao Paolo. He also worked in Turkey, Spain and in the United States. He completed his academic studies in Tokyo and Lyon and speaks seven languages.

Attending the FIS is not cheap. Parents must pay a debenture that is given back when their child graduates. If the fees are paid by a company, the debenture is HK$250,000; if the fees are paid by, the sum is HK$90,000. The annual tuition fees range from HK$106,000 to HK$121,000. French students whose families are in need can apply for scholarships from l'Agence pour l'Enseignement de Francais a l'Etranger (AEFE, Agency for the Teaching of French Overseas). They can also apply for a small number of scholarships provided by the school.

The FIS is a non-profit association run by a twelve-member Council of Administration consisting the parents of the students and representatives of the Consul General of France, the Chamber of Commerce and staff of the schools. Their service is voluntary and unpaid. The Council meets six to eight times a year.

The man chosen chairman of the school board in June 2018 was Clement Brunet-Moret, managing director of ASPAC Distribution Ltd and a resident of Hong Kong for more than twenty years. His two children attended the school. His grandfather began his professional life as a teacher in a small village in southeast France, worked as principal of French lycees abroad and finished his career as director general of National Education. In an interview in February 2019, Brunet-Moret said there were too many French students who were not attending the FIS. "Our objective is to bring them back. We must make the school sufficiently attractive to persuade them come back from the other international schools they are attending. The competition among these schools is intensifying as the number increases. The figures from the Hong Kong Education Bureau show there are too many international schools here." Between 2015 and 2019, 3,693 additional places were created in these schools.

CHAPTER THREE
Italians

The greatest Italian contribution to Hong Kong has been its missionaries. The schools, hospitals, hospices and other welfare institutions they established serve Hong Kong people today — the positive results of colonialism. The government of the time welcomed them for providing these services and contributing to social stability. The British administrators were also comfortable with missionaries who were Christians from Europe — whom they could understand and manage more easily than people of other regions and religions

One of the first to arrive was Italian Franciscan priest Antonio Feliciani, on March 3, 1842, just fourteen months after the British raised their flag over Hong Kong. It was the start of a long and remarkable Italian missionary presence here that has continued until today. Italian priests and nuns laid the foundations of the city's Catholic Church and established schools and hospitals. The two most important Italian missionary orders in the early years of British rule were the Pontifical Institute for Foreign Missions (PIME) and the Order of the Canossian Sisters.

The foreign order which has sent the largest number

EUROPEANS IN HONG KONG

of missionaries to Hong Kong is the PIME; since 1858, 205 missionaries have come, more than ninety percent of them Italian. PIME provided the first leaders of the city's Catholic Church—Apostolic Vicar and then Bishop—from 1874 to 1969. Since then, the Bishop has been a Chinese. The PIME missionaries have founded churches, primary and secondary schools, social service centers, homes for elderly people, food and clothing distribution centers and medical clinics. They have played a key role in establishing the city's Catholic Church and evangelizing its people, especially in the Saikung and Taipo areas of the New Territories. They have worked in close co-operation with Chinese priests, nuns and laity. Before 1949, they also established Catholic churches and communities in the three counties of Guangdong Province next to Hong Kong. They have served, and are serving, as parish priests. In 1977, Father Enea Tapella (達碑立神父) established the Society of Homes for the Handicapped, which has since 2001 been known as Fu Hong (扶康會); today it operates over forty units serving 3,600 people with disabilities every year. From 1968 until 2003, Father Francesco Lerda (力理得神父) was president of Caritas Hong Kong (香港明愛), one of the largest social welfare institutions in the city. It operates over 240 service units from 150 locations; it has more than 5,700 full-time staff, helped by thousands of volunteers, and has an annual budget for recurrent expenditure of more than HK$1.85 billion. Since 1969, a group of PIME priests—including Father Franco Mella—have worked in factories and become active in social causes, including working for boat people, street sleepers and refugees. As of January 2017, there were twenty-nine PIME missionaries serving in Hong Kong. They work as parish priests, teachers, in academia and social welfare and as activists. Globally, it has more 500 missionaries in eighteen countries around the world; its headquarters is in

Rome.

The Pontifical Institute for Foreign Missions (Latin: Pontifium Institutum Missionum Exterarum, PIME) was founded in Milan in 1850. In 1926, Pope Pius XI officially recognized it as PIME. In 1852, the first group of missionaries—seven priests and two lay people—left for a remote island in Melanesia, now Papua New Guinea; it was cut off from the rest of the world and no missionary wanted to go there. After three years, they accepted that the mission had failed. One of the seven, Father Paolo Reina (雷納神父), decided to come to Hong Kong. He was the first PIME priest to arrive in the city, on the morning of April 10, 1858. Three of his colleagues followed him on May 15. Their first duties were to care for the Portuguese and Eurasian Catholic communities and assist soldiers, the sick and inmates of prison. They also prepared to evangelize the Chinese of Hong Kong and Guangdong Province.

One of the three colleagues was Father Giovanni Timoleone Raimondi (高雷門神父), he became the first Apostolic Vicar, the title then used for the Bishop, of Hong Kong in 1874, a position he held until his death in the city on September 27, 1894. He left a great mark on the Catholic Church in Hong Kong, in buildings and organization. He had a strong and demanding personality, this was needed at that time to build the church in a young, frontier colony. He established good relations with the British administration and the orders of Sisters working in Hong Kong. He was a talented fundraiser, at home and overseas. He built St Joseph's Church (聖若瑟堂) in Garden Road, Central, mainly for Irish Catholic soldiers; it opened in November 20, 1872. He raised money from the government, the local Christian community and Jewish donors. It was one of only three Catholic churches at that time. A devastating typhoon in September 1874 destroyed the building; it was rebuilt and opened in 1876. It is one of Father

Raimondi's legacies in Hong Kong. Given its prime location in Central, it is one of the busiest Catholic churches in the city, with ten masses every Sunday and three every day. The services are held in English, Tagalog and Cantonese.

In 1888, he also built the Cathedral of the Immaculate Conception (聖母無原罪主教坐堂); it has been the center of Catholic worship in the city ever since. The church was first built in 1843 in Wellington Street (威靈頓街); it was damaged by a fire in 1859 and rebuilt. In the 1880s, Raimondi deemed the environment not suitable for religious worship; he sold the building to a businessman who demolished it. He ordered the construction of the cathedral on its current site, in Caine Road (堅道). It was consecrated on December 7, 1888, on the eve of the Festival of the Immaculate Conception. He hired a firm of London architects to design a building in Gothic style, with room for more than 1,000 worshippers. It is 62.5 meters long, 18.6 meters wide and 39.6 meters high, excluding the cross on the roof. As Apostolic Vicar, Raimondi organized the city into four ecclesiastical districts; he provided them with the structures they needed. He aggressively promoted Catholic education, making it available to young people, including street children and juvenile delinquents. He lobbied the government for grants for Catholic schools. In 1858, there was one Catholic school with eight boys; by 1874, there were eighteen with 723 students. That is a measure of the impact Bishop Raimondi had on the colony. He invited the La Salle Christian Brothers to manage some of the schools. They arrived on November 7, 1875, and took over the West Point Reformatory and Saint Saviour College, which they renamed St Joseph's College (聖若瑟書院). In the premises on Kennedy Road where it moved in September 1918, St Joseph's has since its foundation been one of the leading secondary schools in the city.

Bishop Raimondi also founded a newspaper, the Hong Kong

Catholic Register, to present the church's views. He died on September 27, 1894. In his *Story of a Hundred Years*, Irish Jesuit Thomas Ryan described Father Raimondi in this way: "it is no exaggeration to say that, from the moment Father Raimondi stepped from the boat in May 1858, the future of the Church in the Colony, and of the PIME's part in establishing it, was assured. He brought courage and massive strength, he inspired confidence as only a born leader can do. The years of uncertainty were at the end. When he died thirty-six years later, his work was done. Its fruits remained." At the time of his death, the diocese had one seminary and thirty-six colleges and regular schools. He served for one year as head of the seminary. Between its foundation in 1841 and his death in 1894, fifteen Chinese priests served in Hong Kong.

He was succeeded as Apostolic Vicar by another PIME missionary, Luigi Piazzoli (和主教). He took over the post on January 11, 1895. A different personality to his predecessor; he was quiet and modest. His greatest service came in helping the victims of bubonic plague in 1894: pastoral work in Kowloon: and evangelizing people in the Mainland. On August 4, 1904, he left Hong Kong for Italy to seek medical treatment for a high fever and other illnesses. He died in a Milan hospital on December 26 that year. He was succeeded by Bishop Domenico Pozzoni (師多敏主教), who held the post for twenty years, until his death in February 1924, aged sixty-two. A total of 10,000 people attended his funeral. In its obituary, the South China Morning Post said: "His Lordship's great interest in education, his welfare work and his public spirit contributed to a full record of service such as entitle him to public thanks and a worthy funeral... His charm of manner, his innate kindliness, his self-sacrifice for others have won for him more than mere respect, something which converts mere regret into poignant grief." He was a strong supporter of the University of Hong Kong, which opened in March 1912. He was on the Court, its governing body, and played an active role in its management. At the time of his death, the city had 28,110 Catholics out of a population of 650,000, with sixty-five churches and 367 chapels. There were twenty PIME missionaries, ten Chinese priests and 131 European and thirty-five Chinese nuns.

Enrico Pascal Valtorta (恩理覺) served as the last Apostolic Vicar and first Bishop of Hong Kong, between March 8, 1926, and September 3, 1951. He lived in Hong Kong for forty-four years, including the Calvary of World War II. Ordained as a priest in Milan on March 30, 1907, he arrived in Hong Kong on October 5 that year. After working as a missionary in San On County (新安縣) in Guangdong and Sai Kung (西貢區), he served in Hong Kong churches and as chaplain to Victoria Gaol. His most difficult period was World War II, including the Japanese Occupation from December 1941 to August 1945. He organized priests and nuns as volunteers to help the tens of thousands of refugees who poured into the city from July 1937. On June 10, 1940, Italy declared war on Great Britain. The Governor told Valtorta that only one Italian priest could be left in each parish, in addition to those working in the bishop's house. He allowed all Italian nuns to continue their work. So four PIME priests went to Macao and three to the Mainland. After the Japanese capture of Hong Kong in December 1941, Italy had suddenly become an ally of the ruling power. The Italian priests were free to work as they wish but the sixty nuns and priests of "hostile nations" were interned on January 5, 1942. Conditions in the city deteriorated dramatically. Tens of thousands fled to Macao or the Mainland. Every morning city officials collected corpses lying on the street. "Famished people die in the streets," wrote Valtorta. "There might even be some cases of cannibalism. There is no way to help. We try to organize some rescue committees in the parishes, but our resources are so limited. Yet, somehow, we hope to help as many families as possible to overcome these unspeakable hardships." In September 1943, Italy signed an armistice with the Allies—and suddenly became an enemy of Japan. Despite this, the Japanese authorities allowed the Italian priests and nuns to continue their work in Hong Kong. This was because of the high esteem in which they held Valtorta.

The Apostolic Vicariate of Hong Kong was upgraded to Bishop in April 1946. Valtorta was installed as the First Bishop on October 31, 1948. During his time as bishop, he set up scholastic and charitable institutions and welfare centers. He had good relations with the British government. He died in Hong Kong on September 3, 1951. He is remembered today in Valtorta College (恩主教書院), the former Taipo Catholic Secondary School, which opened in September 1976; it is a subsidized Anglo-Chinese co-educational secondary school.

After the new government took power in China in 1949, they expelled all the foreign missionaries, including those of PIME. China's loss was Hong Kong's gain. While some missionaries went to Taiwan, the majority went to Hong Kong. Some were assigned by their orders to new missions overseas, but many stayed in Hong Kong. Their knowledge of the Chinese people and their languages was invaluable. By 1957, the city's Catholic Church had thirteen male congregations, with 279 priests and brothers and twenty female congregations with 565 nuns. Among those expelled was Father Lorenzo Bianchi (白英奇神父), a priest in Haifeng (海豐) in Guangdong Province. On October 9, 1949, he had been consecrated Coadjutor Bishop in the Hong Kong cathedral by Bishop Valtorta, making him number two. A week later, he returned to Haifeng, where he had worked for seventeen years. On Easter Saturday 1950, he was arrested. On the death of Bishop Valtorta in September 1951, Bianchi became the new

Bishop of Hong Kong—but he was in prison. He did not know if he would survive; he was already 52. On October 17, 1952, he was set free and crossed the Lo Wu Bridge—in the morning a prisoner, in the afternoon the leader of the city's Catholics. When he reached Kowloon station at 2100 that day, nearly 1,000 of the faithful had gathered there to welcome him. He was installed as Bishop on October 26 that year.

The 1950s and 1960s was a period of intense activity for the PIME priests, as it was for all the religious orders. They played an essential role in providing schools, medical care and social services for the hundreds of thousands of refugees who poured into Hong Kong from the Mainland. In 1953, the church founded the Catholic Social Welfare Conference of the Hong Kong diocese; on October 1, 1961, it was renamed Caritas-Hong Kong (香港明愛). It has since become one of the largest providers of social welfare in the city. There was a rapid increase in the number of Catholic believers, with 6,000 baptisms in 1956 alone.

On November 30, 1968, Bianchi resigned as Bishop; he was 69. The number of Chinese priests and lay members had grown dramatically over the previous twenty years. It was time to appoint a Chinese bishop. "But the Holy See was reluctant to grant full power to his successor, Father Francis Hsu (徐誠斌神父), who was named only Apostolic Administrator ,instead of Ordinary of the diocese," wrote Gianni Criveller in *From Milan to Hong Kong, 150 years of Mission*, the official history of the PIME in the city. "This unforeseen development triggered sadness and bewilderment in Hong Kong, especially among the Chinese clergy, the laity and Bishop Bianchi himself ...It seemed as though the Holy See could not fully trust the Chinese clergy. In April 1969, Bishop Bianchi left Hong Kong, went to the Vatican and was apparently able to lobby Pope Paul VI, a fellow citizen of Brescia, to redress the injustice against Father Hsu." On May

29, he was nominated Ordinary Bishop and invested on October 26 as the first Chinese bishop of Hong Kong. This marked the official end of PIME holding this most senior post in Hong Kong, with four bishops since 1875. Since then, all the bishops have been Chinese.

In September 1968, the Missionary Sisters of the Immaculate, also known as the PIME Sisters, arrived in Hong Kong. The year 1972 marked the highest number of PIME priests in the city — seventy-one. That year, PIME priests and Sisters opened homes for the elderly in Tsuen Wan and Tsing Yi. In 1977, Father Enea Tapella founded the Society of Homes for the Handicapped; since 2001, it has been called the Fu Hong Society.

The Second Vatican Council of 1962-65 was landmark. It took decisions aimed at bringing the Catholic Church closer to ordinary people — including the use of the vernacular language instead of Latin, the priest facing the congregation and simplifying prayers and the liturgical calendar. The impact of the Council was felt around the world, including among the fathers of the PIME in Hong Kong. A split emerged among them as to the best way forward. The majority, mainly the older priests, believed they should continue their traditional forms of work — pastoral, educational and social welfare work in the parishes and schools. A smaller group, about a dozen, believed that they should become involved in social and political issues, fighting for justice with the oppressed, the poor and marginalized. They wanted to live with the poor, the homeless and boat people. This group founded the Social Concern Group of the PIME. If this meant taking part in political protest, then they would do so. Six went to work in factories, part- or full-time. In 1980, two went to live on a boat in Yau Ma Tei typhoon shelter; they lived there for ten years. They organized social and educational initiatives for children and young people in the fishing community. When thousands of Vietnamese refugees arrived in the 1980s, some PIME missionaries visited the camps where they were placed and lobbied the government for better treatment of them.

The handover of Hong Kong to China on July 1, 1997 was a watershed, for the PIME priests as it was for everyone else. Should they stay or should they leave? After the events that followed the establishment of the new government in the Mainland in 1949, many Catholics in Hong Kong were afraid. Thousands chose to emigrate to countries where religious freedom was guaranteed. The PIME priests made their position clear. In 1985, one year after the Sino-British Joint Declaration on Hong Kong, they issued a document stating that they intended to stay in the city after 1997, no matter what happened. They reaffirmed this decision in 1993: "a few years ago, after a lengthy discussion among ourselves, we decided to let the faithful know that we were determined not to leave Hong Kong in view of the year 1997. That decision made back then proved to be a truly missionary choice. It is influencing our pastoral ministry in the present. We want to remain by our people. We want to journey with them." The church celebrated the handover with a solemn celebration at the Cathedral. All the members of PIME attended. At that time there were forty-four assigned to the Hong Kong mission, forty-three priests and one lay missionary. Their median age was over sixty. Of them, thirty-three priests were working in Hong Kong, three in Taiwan and two in the Mainland. Three were in Italy for health reasons and one had been newly assigned to the mission.

On July 4, 1999, the first new Catholic Church built after the handover opened in Tsing Yi. Since the 1970s, PIME priests had worked in Tsing Yi, to develop the Catholic community. They established homes for the elderly; one was principal of a local Catholic school. Since 1997, the PIME priests have continued their work; new fathers have arrived to join them.

As of 2021, there were thirty PIME missionaries serving in Hong Kong work as parish priests, teachers, in academia and social welfare and as activists. The earliest of them arrived in Hong Kong in 1955. That is less than half the peak of seventy-one in 1972. This decrease is a result of a fall in vocations in Italy — as in the rest of Western Europe — and the increasing strength of the Chinese church and civil society; they have taken over responsibilities held before by PIME. The priests who come make a lifetime commitment to the city. They will serve as long as their health permits and their presence is allowed by the government.

Father Quirino de Ascaniis (江志堅神父) spent seventy-six years in the Mainland and Hong Kong, the longest of any PIME priest. He passed away on January 11, 2009, at the House for the Elderly run by the Little Sisters of the Poor in Hong Kong; he was a hundred years old. After a funeral mass, he was buried in Hong Kong. More than forty priests and hundreds of the faithful attended the funeral Mass. In his address, Bishop John Tong (湯漢主教) said: "In many instances, he found death when he came to China to serve the mission during the Second World War, but, responding to the Lord's call, he never backed out."

He was born in Teramo (泰拉莫) in central Italy on August 5, 1908. He was ordained as a priest in Milan on September 24, 1932 and left for Hong Kong in August 1933. After studying Cantonese, he was sent in 1936 to Huiyang (惠陽) in Guangdong Province. In December 1941, fighting forced him to leave the area; but he returned soon after and remained there until he was expelled in October 1951. In Hong Kong, he served as Rector of the Diocesan Seminary in Sai Kung and Rector of the same district until 1961. From 1961, he served as assistant pastor at Saint Teresa in Kowloon and, from 1966 to 1993, assistant pastor in the Church of the Holy Rosary and chaplain of Queen Elizabeth Hospital. In 1993, he retired to the Saint Joseph's Rest Home.

EUROPEANS IN HONG KONG

In 2018, Chorabooks published his diary *Revixit Spiritus Meus: Notes from a Missionary in China* in Italian, as an e-book and paperback. This is how he describes the start of his vocation: "the mission is a 'heroism of holiness'. Heroism, because the missionary leaves everything and everyone to be close to those who are far from him and far from what for him is the most precious: the Christian faith. The missionary is not a benefactor, a psychologist, a sociologist or an anthropologist; the missionary is a man of God who goes on a mission to bring God and, as a consequence, also the good derived from Western civilization, from its Catholic matrix, then art, science and culture."

The best known PIME priest in Hong Kong today is Franco Mella. He was just eight years old when he decided to become a priest. Born in 1948, in Milan, he had been to his weekly Sunday Catholic class and he told his mother: "I said 'I want to be like that priest'. And then she phoned all the relatives and said, 'Franco wants to become a priest', so every time I went to see my aunt, my uncle, my cousins, 'Ah,' they said, 'you're going to the seminary'."

He arrived in Hong Kong in 1974, having already been involved in workers' rights in his native Italy. He spent more than twenty years working with children with disabilities in the Mainland, but was thrown out in 2011, which he puts down to a disagreement between China and the Holy See. But he says he is now permitted to return. Now his main work is with the city's asylum seekers, providing education opportunities that can assist them when they head to third countries. The weekly timetable includes lessons in various languages, practical skills, and handicrafts, some taught by former refugees, and the asylum seekers are left to choose which lessons they would like to attend. "There are about eighty refugees coming for the lessons they are interested in and about eighty per cent of the teachers are refugees themselves," said Mella. "Some volunteers from Hong Kong teach Mandarin or Cantonese. We have a Chilean Sister who teaches Spanish and a Swiss Pastor who is teaching German. Some of us are teaching Italian—Latin and guitar and other lessons."

Mella has spent the past five decades in this region caring for those that society tends to neglect. And he has never been afraid to go up against a factory's management or government authorities to fight for better conditions. During the 1970s, he and other PIME priests went to work in factories in San Po Kong and Tsuen Wan among other areas at a time when these facilities could often be dangerous. Workers would die or be injured in fires. As well as working in garment and other factories, Mella would demand better conditions from the management.

He recalls being sacked from three factories. "I worked in fourteen factories," he said. "So garment factories, electronic factories, bag factories, and I was dismissed three times especially because we were very concerned about safety in the working place. At that time, there were fires in the factories and people would die and we would complain about that and be dismissed." While his co-workers would be initially curious about this Italian working alongside them, he says, when they realized he spoke fluent Cantonese, then they would treat him as one of their own. "I remember my first pay was fifteen Hong Kong dollars per day and, after six months, they raised my salary by fifty cents," he said, adding that the pay also meant that, as a priest, he was not dependent on the PIME order but could be self-sufficient.

In 1980, he went to live in Yau Ma Tei typhoon shelter on a boat for what would be ten years. The fishermen often married Mainland wives, who were allowed to come to Hong Kong to live on the boats but were not permitted on land, in wat was known as the "boat brides" issue. This presented difficulties when they needed medical care, gave birth, or later their young children needed someone to accompany them to school. In February 1986, Mella invited the press to the typhoon shelter and the following month started a hunger strike. After a few days, the government agreed to provide papers for 2,000 "boat brides".

The award-winning 1999 drama movie *Ordinary Heroes*, directed by Hong Kong director Ann Hui, focused on the work of Mella and a fellow priest in assisting the Yau Ma Tei typhoon shelter families. In 2018, Hong Kong filmmaker Kong King-chu also screened a documentary he had created about the life and work of the Italian priest. *Father Mella* was shown at the Indie Film Fest.

After Yau Ma Tei, Mella then went to live among the city's street sleepers. How can people simply walk past people living on the streets, he asks, without noticing their plight? He also explained how, since the street sleepers were ignored under bridges and overpasses, he felt they should go and sleep outside district offices, to demand housing for them and make their situation more visible. By giving them their own accommodation, he said, you can turn many lives around. "If they are considered as human beings, then many things can change."

After the handover in June 1997, a key campaign for Mella was the issue of right of abode for children of Hong Kong citizens born in the Mainland, one that still has not been entirely resolved. The government voiced fears that too many people would be allowed into Hong Kong; it led the government to ask the National People's Congress Standing Committee for its first reinterpretation of the Basic Law.

The number cited, says Mella, was an exaggeration. In the early 2000s, it led to sit-ins, hunger strikes and demonstrations. In 2000, the PIME priests set up the Right of Abode University, their first school for these children who were not allowed to study or work in Hong Kong. The school was based on the teachings and example of an Italian Catholic priest, whom Mella sees as a key influence. Lorenzo Milani believed education should be for poor as well as rich children and he was also an advocate of conscientious objection. When he was banished to a remote mountain village, Barbiana in Italy, in 1954, Milani set up a school, where, with his pupils he wrote "Letter to a Teacher" denouncing an education system that ignored the poor. Pope Francis prayed at his grave in 2017. In his work, Mella echoes Milani's belief in equality in education and helping those in society who are disadvantaged.

Canossian Sisters

The other Italian religious order that has greatly contributed to Hong Kong is the Canossian Daughters of Charity, who first arrived in 1860. Their mission was and is "Education, Pastoral Work, Medical and Social Welfare Work, according to the needs of the time and the places". In the 160 years since then, they have founded primary and secondary schools, including one for children with visual impairment, one for children with hearing impairment, a Good Shepherd Home, commercial and evening schools, free schools, a hospital. They have taken care of tens of thousands of orphan girls and trained them for life and work in society: and provided medical and pastoral care to the elderly, the sick and the needy.

To mark the 160th anniversary of their arrival on April 12, 2020, Clemente Contestabile, Consul General of Italy, wrote a letter to the *South China Morning Post*. "The six nuns arrived in Hong Kong from Italy after a long and perilous journey. Their mission: to bring education and health care to the poorest people in the British colony. They were young, brave and capable... With the strength of their faith and their determination, the young women brought hope and relief to many in Hong Kong in the face of epidemics, natural disasters and a challenging social environment. Today the message of peace, care and solidarity carried by those six young Italian women in 1860 still resonates strongly in Hong Kong. It is a powerful source of inspiration for us all in a critical time for Hong Kong, Italy and the whole world."

In the early years, the Sisters came from Italy and other countries in Europe. Later Chinese women joined. In 1922, the group of the Canossian Tertiary Sisters was asked by the Bishop of the Hong Kong Diocese to become an independent religious congregation of the Diocese: the Congregation of the Sisters of the Precious Blood. In the Canossian Sisters group, since 1991, the Provincial Superior has been a Chinese Sister. Today there are eighty-five Sisters, of whom seventy-one are Chinese. They operate twenty kindergarten, primary and secondary schools, with more than 16,000 students.

The order was founded in 1808 by St Magdalene of Canossa (1774-1835), daughter of the noble family of Canossa in Verona, northern Italy. She set up free schools for children of the poor, to teach them skills that would enable them to earn a decent living. In 1822, she established training schools to prepare young women to teach poor girls in rural areas. The order always aimed to take the Christian message overseas. Hong Kong was the first destination; six Sisters arrived here on April 12, 1860. On May 1, they started the English and Portuguese section of the Italian Convent School, with forty pupils. On May 10, they started the Pui Ching Chinese School and orphanage in the same compound. From Hong Kong, the order later sent missions to China, Macao, India, Timor, Malaysia, Singapore, Philippines, Japan and Australia.

When the six Sisters stepped off the boat, full of expectation and uncertainty, they were met later that same evening by an elegant British woman who was to become an unlikely partner in their mission. This was Emily Aloysia Bowring, daughter of Sir John Bowring, governor of Hong Kong from 1854 to 1859. He was a Unitarian; his church rejected many tenets of the Catholic religion. Of his nine children, three converted to Catholicism, a matter of great tension within the family. Before Sir John moved to Hong Kong, Emily converted; she was devout and talked of becoming a nun. In 1854, with her parents and one sister, she moved to Hong Kong. She worked here among the poor and sick, which reflected well on her father among the Chinese population; she learned Cantonese. Her family was gifted linguistically—her siblings were fluent in French, German, Sanskrit and Arabic. Emily spoke French and some Italian and Portuguese. When her father and sister returned to England in 1859, she decided to become a nun and remain in Hong Kong. Sir John was distraught—his own wife had died only a few months before and he feared he would never see Emily again.

After their exhausting voyage from Europe, the six Sisters were delighted to meet Emily. They soon realized that this refined and highly educated woman was a gift from God. They needed to learn everything—from English and Cantonese to the climate and life, culture and beliefs of Chinese in Hong Kong. In front of them was a woman who could greatly help them—she had lived in Hong Kong since 1854 and knew the city well, both rich and poor. She entered the order on April 29, 1860, and became the first head mistress of the Italian Convent School in Caine Road; today it is the Sacred Heart Canossian School (嘉諾撒聖心學校). She took her vows on March 29, 1862. In becoming a nun, she changed her lifestyle radically. In the Governor's mansion, she was waited on by servants who prepared her clothes, made her meals and transported her around the city; she met the colonial elite and could expect a life of ease and comfort with a husband from the same class. Now she was living in humid and overcrowded quarters, with a ceaseless load of teaching and pastoral duties. The colonial society to which she had belonged before regarded her with shock and incomprehension. She served as headmistress until she fell sick in the first week of August 1870. She had a fever but was able to attend evening prayers. On the August 19, the fever became more severe and she died the next day; she was just thirty-seven. In its obituary on August 21, the Hong Kong Chronicle said that Emily was "well known and universally respected since the year 1859 when her father retired from the Governorship, leaving her to work in the Catholic Mission which she had chosen for her field of labor." She was the sixth Canossian Sister to be buried in the St Michael's Catholic Cemetery at Happy Valley—in a mission of only ten years. Sir John Bowring paid for the erection of stone crosses for her and the other deceased Sisters at the cemetery plot of the Canossian Sisters.

The work of the Sisters quickly extended beyond education. They took in many orphan girls abandoned by their families. By September 1863, their orphanage was looking after forty-eight; more were asking for admission every week. In 1869, the Sisters opened in Wanchai a Good Shepherd Home to help girls escape from prostitution; they set up St Francis Hospital for the poor, and St Francis School with English, Portuguese and Chinese sections.

The care of orphan girls became a major part of the work. Between 1893 and 1943, the Sisters looked after 84,150 such girls and provided medical care to tens of thousands. In 1897, the Sisters opened a Chinese primary school in the fast-growing village of Aberdeen. By 1910, the fiftieth anniversary of their arrival, the number of Sisters had grown to sixty-seven, teaching

1,180 students, of whom 646 were Chinese and 349 were orphans, and caring for 857 others.

In 1929, a benefactor named Mr Stephens donated to the Canossian Sisters a piece of land at 1 Old Peak Road. Canossa Hospital began with sixteen beds: It was destroyed during the World War II. After the war, the Sisters started to rebuild a five-story building on the same site. The brand new hospital was completed in 1960 as a private, non-profit organization with 160 beds, including a ward reserved for the poor. From 1972 to 1974, a new wing was added increasing the number of beds to 196. In June 1991, the Sisters entrusted the management of the hospital to Caritas Hong Kong; they continue to work as nursing staff and pastoral care workers, to provide quality holistic care to the community, in the spirit of Christ.

Under the corporate management of Caritas Hong Kong, a brand new block was built in 2013; also the old block was renovated into a modernized hospital in 2017. The whole hospital was totally transformed into a state-of-act and modernized healthcare organization with the following facilities: a well-equipped Operating Theater; a Special Care Unit; a CSSD with T-Doc System; Endoscopy Unit; a Maternity Unit with an Operating Theater for caesarean section; a fully equipped Clinical Laboratory Department; Department of Diagnostic and Imaging (DDI); Pharmacy; Physiotherapy Department; Dietetic Department; Infection Control Unit; Quality & Risk Department; and a Child Health Center and other additions.

In 2018, Canossa Hospital had a joint venture with Hong Kong Asia Hospital Limited to set up a Cardiac Center with a Cardiac Catheterization & Intervention Laboratory on the G/F of the old building, this clinic is now in operation to provide treatment to patients with heart problems. In the same year, a drug reconstitution room was approved by Department of Health for preparing drugs for chemotherapy. A new Orthopedics Center was opened on March 1, 2019.

The Canossian Sisters and staff are committed to:

- Maintain Catholic medical ethics in the treatment of the patients;
- Offer holistic care;
- Provide safe and quality health services for the local community;
- Promote wellness;
- Work in partnerships with patient groups and health care agencies.

The communist revolution of 1949 brought unprecedented challenges to the Sisters, as it did to all the Religious Orders. All their members were expelled from China; the last to arrive, M Angelina Ranzini arrived on September 4, 1952. She had been based in Guluba (古路壩) in Shaanxi Province (陝西省).

The flood of refugees from the Mainland led to enormous demand for housing and education. The Sisters stepped up to the challenge. By August 1958, more than 10,000 students were attending their schools, out of 400,000 students in the whole city. Their and other mission schools played a critical role in the transformation of Hong Kong and its people. The majority of the students were children of refugees. Because of the anti-Japanese and civil wars, their parents had limited opportunity for formal education. They arrived in Hong Kong with no more than they could carry. Many lived in makeshift housing on the side of hills or mountains or in small, crowded apartments provided by the government. This was not a good environment for young people to study. But the schools provided a modern, disciplined and moral education, in English and Chinese, at a modest fee. Once the students entered the school premises, they could forget the poverty and shortages in which they lived. They could learn the same subjects that were taught to students in Europe and North America and join the modern world. They had a strong motivation to learn, to have a better life than their parents. The graduates of these schools went on to work in the government, private companies, law, medicine, teaching and other professions. They helped to create the economic miracle that transformed Hong Kong from an entrepôt into a manufacturing powerhouse and then a global financial and business center. The Canossian schools have strong and active alumnae associations—evidence of the gratitude which they feel for their alma mater and the awareness of what they owe them.

In the 1960s, the Sisters opened in Wanchai the Canossian School for Visually Disabled, which closed in 1985, after 25 years, also a home for elderly visually disabled women. In 1973, the Canossa School for the Deaf was opened and renamed Caritas Magdalene School in 1990 and closed in 2007. The Sacred Heart Canossian Commercial School later renamed Sacred Heart Canossian College of Commerce started in 1905 and was closed in 2014.

In 1964, the Sisters were given management of the Caritas Medical Center in Kowloon, which opened on December 17 that year, with 500 beds. In May 1977, the Sisters withdrew from the administration of Caritas Medical Center after thirteen years. The hospital had grown too large for them and they did not have enough Sisters with specialized training. They continued to work in the hospital, as nurses and providing pastoral care. By 1988, the number of Canossian schools in Hong Kong and Macao had increased, with more than 25,000 students. There were 170 Sisters, half of them Chinese.

EUROPEANS IN HONG KONG

By the 1960s, the economies of Western Europe had recovered from World War II and were growing steadily, in Italy as in other countries. Universal education opened new work and career opportunities for women who had not existed for their mothers and grandmothers. The number of vocations started to fall sharply. To become a nun and devote your life to chastity, obedience and the service of others is no easy choice. The situation was similar in Hong Kong. The 'economic miracle' and the high levels of education achieved by women gave them many new choices. The number choosing to become religious declined. This drop of vocations significantly affected the work of the Sisters. They could not continue such a diversity of projects and had to withdraw from some of them. At the same time, Hong Kong was training a growing number of doctors, teachers, social workers and other professionals who could manage well the Sisters' schools, hospitals and other institutions.

On October 2, 1988, Pope John Paul II canonized Magdalene of Canossa, the founder of the Order. He especially praised her humility and charity.

Community Grew Slowly
From 1861, the Kingdom of Italy had a representative in Hong Kong, of whom the first six were British. The first professional diplomat, Eugenio Zanoni Volpicelli, arrived in 1899 as Consul General and stayed for twenty years. During and after World War II, from 1942 to 1949, the diplomatic office was closed. Since 1950, the country has been represented in Hong Kong by a professional diplomat.

After World War II, the Italian community was small. By the late 1970s, it numbered 300 to 400.They they worked in banking, food and wine and managed shops. With the start of China's open-door policy, the number of Italian individuals and companies has increased. In the early 1990s, there were just over 1,000 Italians; today about 4,000 Italians live in the SAR. Companies include luxury goods producers like Bulgari and Salvatore Ferragamo, solicitors de Bedin & Lee, banks like Intesa SanPaolo and Unicredit and importers of wine and food. The Italian Chamber of Commerce was established in 1997. Italians work in many professions — finance, business, fashion, hotels, restaurants, transportation, logistics, accounting, design, architecture, teaching, arts, music, NGOs and food and wine. Many recent arrivals are young professionals looking for overseas experience; they work in fashion, food and beverage, automotives, logistics and design. All share the shock of Hong Kong's fast pace and dynamism compared to life at home. As one of them, Valeria Maisto Wright, put it vividly, "Life in Hong Kong is like the life of a dog; one year here equals seven years in Italy."

The Italian Women's Association was set up in 1996. It holds social gatherings and cultural activities, playgroups for children, excursions and lectures. It is especially helpful for those who have just arrived in Hong Kong. It raises money for charities in Hong Kong and Macao. In 2004, the Scuola Italiana Manzoni was established, to provide Italian-language classes for children aged 4 to 14, on Saturday mornings. Since then, it has grown to become the largest Italian school in Asia. It is funded by individual donors and sponsors. Honorary president Eligio Oggionni said, "Having our own school, even if only for a few hours a week, is vitally important. In fact, it is only thanks to this that we can guarantee our children supplementary courses in writing, listening and speaking, as well as the study of our history and geography. This, in my opinion, remains the most effective means of keeping alive in their hearts the love for our distant homeland." The Marco Polo Society is the Association of

Friendship between Hong Kong and Italy.

Ugo Conta was a well-known Italian restaurateur, musician and judo trainer, among few of his skills, in the sixty years that he decided to make Hong Kong his home until his death in 2020 from Covid-19 in his native town of Mantua, Italy.

"He was a natural maître'd," says radio and film producer Garry Pollard, who would regularly visit the Italian restaurants Rigoletto, later Ugo's. His former chef said he was a colorful character who created a taste of his northern Italian food in Hong Kong at a time when there were few Italian restaurants. Conta put a great emphasis on the standard of the food provided and on the restaurant décor to ensure that people felt as if they were sitting in an Italian taverna.

He came to Hong Kong in 1962 and would play drums with a jazz quartet at The Den in the Hilton Hotel. He also played piano and organ, particularly later at his restaurant Ugo's, set up in 2002. He would sit down at an organ there to entertain the guests. In the last fifteen years or so of his life, following on from Ugo's, he ran the May Chau Music Academy in Mid-Levels with his talented singer and musician wife, May Chau.

Another passion was teaching judo—Conta had a center for that but would also teach judo at Hong Kong schools. He was permanently busy, but seems to have thrived on excelling in different areas.

Rigoletto was named after the Italian opera in three acts by Giuseppe Verdi. The red plastic drink stirrers at the Italian restaurant on Fenwick Street in Wan Chai, had a figurine of the jester Rigoletto at the top and were toys for Michelle Chan—daughter of the head chef—to play with as a child. Chan Haksui, age 67, worked with Conta on and off for thirty-five years—joining him first in the kitchen in 1972 at La Bella Donna on Gloucester Road, later joining Rigoletto in 1976. Conta was in business in Rigoletto with several others before setting up his own restaurant. "He was a very dedicated, ambitious person," recalls Chan. "If he was determined to do something, he would do his very best to accomplish it. He was very goal-orientated. He treated me like a brother and [aside from the cooking] I learned judo with him."

Michelle Chan, these days a producer at Radio 3, RTHK, had never been to Europe as a young child. Rigoletto for her was a wonderful place with a big fish tank and a sense of Italy. "Ugo was from Mantua in Italy," she said. "He brought to Hong Kong his hometown food, so he introduced North Italian food to the customers. For me, Rigoletto looked like Italy. It had vintage Italian Roman-style furnishing with red bricks. I remember it as a young child like it was a castle. My first fine dining experience. I had never been to Europe before as a kid but I felt I was in Europe. The decorations felt like I was in Italy. There was a giant fish tank that separated the dining area from the bar. There were also drapes and flags."

In 2002 Conta launched his own restaurant, Ugo's. "Ugo took me to Italy, and flew me first-class on Cathay Pacific," says Chan. There he taught Chan how to cook in his northern Italian style. Conta, he says, was a celebrity in his hometown. "He wasn't a quiet person," she said. "He was lively and loved to socialize with the customers. His menu was all handwritten. In Ugo's, we made our own pasta and ravioli. He made sure his nine or so staff rotated in different roles—cooking, cutting the meat, dessert. Everybody had to try different roles."

"He would never sit down and read a book on a sofa," says Luigi Grisi, who came to Hong Kong in 1988 and was a long-term friend of Conta here. Grisi headed up the Dante Alighieri Society in Hong Kong, for a time promoting Italian language and culture. With actress and lawyer Susan Lavender, who is half-

Italian, he also organized for a number of years, starting in the year 2000 to celebrate the Millennium, an annual Italian business and cultural event, "Italy: Quality & Lifestyle" on behalf of the Italian Chamber of Commerce in Hong Kong. Luigi was Vice President of the Italian Chamber at the time.

Conta, Grisi says, enjoyed cultural events and was generous with his time and knowledge. "It was more important to him to promote Italian culture and music than to promote his own restaurant. That kind of approach I liked a lot and I worked very well with him. He had such a dynamic personality."

Conta would choose the music at his restaurants, usually Italian opera. At Rigoletto's, Chan recalls meeting Sophia Loren, also Roger Moore and Sean Connery. "The tycoons often came to Ugo's," says Chan. "The Sun Hung Kai bosses, the Kwoks, plus Richard Li and Cecil Chao. The former Director of Broadcasting for RTHK Cheung Man-yee was also a regular customer," says Chan, "they all liked Italian food."

"I still have a photo of me in Rigoletto as a toddler, says Michelle Chan. "Ugo would carry me in his arms. I only spoke Cantonese as a child, so I'd just say hello and goodbye. One Christmas I had a plastic hammer as a toy, and Ugo would take off his glasses and let me knock the top of his nose with my hammer." Ugo Conta was a stickler for certain rules, says Chan. No children under the age of 12 were allowed. "He was a very passionate man, very warm, especially to the ladies," says Chan, laughing.

In an autobiographical piece, the late Ugo Conta wrote in a book about the Italian community here, about his arrival with his band in Hong Kong on June 28, 1963. "After one day's rest in preparation of our debut, we began playing at the Den Bar. We were welcomed by a large international audience. I saw some extremely beautiful and attractive women, wearing cheongsam, the body-hugging traditional dress with slits at the sides high to the hips, high enough for us, Italian musicians, to lose our heads."

Another Italian who has made a great contribution is Giuseppe Salaroli (羅友聖).He arrived in Hong Kong in 1967 as a missionary of PIME. He worked for several years as a supervisor of a school in Tai O. After a few years, he decided to start a family; in May 1974, he received a dispensation from the Pope to become a layman. On August 10, 1975, he married a Hong Kong Chinese lady at the Church of the Rosary in Hong Kong. They moved to Tai Koo Shing, where he worked as an estate manager. Gifted at organizing events, he developed a strong network with local residents. In 1983, they elected him as their District Councillor for six consecutive terms until 2007 — a total of twenty-four years. He was the only Italian, and only European, to be elected to such an office. For his service, he received two medals, one in 1995 from the last British governor, Chris Patten, and the second, the Medal of Honor, in 2002 from the first Chief Executive, Tung Chee-hwa.

The PIME and the Canossian Sisters were the largest religious orders to come from Italy, but were not the only ones. In October 1927, Salesians of Dom Bosco (鮑思高慈幼會) Fathers arrived from Macao and opened the Saint Louis Industrial School (聖類斯工藝學校) in Aberdeen. In 1930, they settled in Shau Kei Wan, where their main Mission House (慈幼會修院) in Hong Kong remains. Two extensions to the house were built from 1932 to 1939. In 1935, they expanded their work in education by founding the Aberdeen Industrial School (香港仔兒 童工藝院). In 1952, they were joined by Salesian Sisters, who had previously served in Shaozhou (now Shaoguan) in Guangdong Province since 1923. They set up Our Lady's College in Wong Tai Sin. Today the order has many projects, including youth centers, publishing, a house

EUROPEANS IN HONG KONG

of studies, a retreat house, a learning house, two parish churches and a vocation office.

The expulsion of foreign missionaries from the Mainland after 1949 brought to Hong Kong many Italian Franciscan friars, among them Gabriele Maria Allegra. He made the first complete translation of the Catholic Bible into Chinese, a task that took him forty years. It remains the official version used in churches in Hong Kong, Macao, Taiwan and the Mainland. Born in Catania in 1907, he went to Hunan Province in 1931, learned Chinese and began his translation. He continued this monumental work during World War II, with the aid of Chinese Franciscan friars. In 1948, they published the first three volumes of the Old Testament and the whole work completed on Christmas Day in 1968. After his expulsion from the Mainland, he lived mostly in Hong Kong, where he died on January 26, 1976. Also serving in Hong Kong after expulsion from the Mainland was a small number of Italian Jesuits.

For thirty-eight years, an Italian institution awaited your visit to the Mandarin Oriental Hong Kong. The ebullient persona of Italian Giovanni Valenti welcomed you with a wide smile, debonair cravat and tails. As the Chief Concierge, Valenti met a host of the rich and famous, though in a hallmark of his distinguished—but discreet—career, he reveals little of their personal details. Suffice it to say, coming through the doors were the British actor Michael Caine, American actor Kevin Costner and, the Iron Lady herself—[the late] British Prime Minister Margaret Thatcher, among many others.

Born in 1944 in Messina, in the northeast of Sicily, Valenti was one of a pair of twins; his twin sister did not survive. It was wartime and Valenti indicates there may have not been enough food. "I have two older sisters and one younger brother," he says, while looking through photographs of his family as he sits in an opulent armchair in the Mandarin lobby. This was his home for nearly four decades; while he never lived within the premises, his life revolved around the needs of the guests that came through its doors.

"It's all about attitude," said Valenti. "Never, never, never contradict a guest." At seventy-eight (as of 2022), Valenti was a tanned picture of health, who regularly plays tennis at the Ladies Recreation Club and is a past trophy winner. Able to converse in a number of languages, he would fluidly swap into the language of the guests to attend to their needs or iron out any wrinkles to their enjoyment. He oversaw more than seventy staff members and a fleet of luxury cars. But on the rare occasions when a guest became too aggressive, he says, then another member of staff would dart over, saying, "Sir, you are needed, overseas call", and Valenti would retire to his quarters and not come out.

Valenti left Sicily as a child, spending his younger years in Florence. His compulsory national service in the Italian army was spent in Perugia and Sardinia "which I loved". Prior to the army, he worked in a shoe shop, Sutor Mantellassi, an opportunity to start practising English with American tourists, he says. "Size eight and a half, narrow, Sir? You know, all this rubbish." Once he had finished his national service, he returned to the shoe shop but, in 1966, there was a flood in Florence. His family lost all their belongings and he lost his sales job. He decided 'enough was enough' and left Italy for London the following year.

An aunt had married an Englishman, so Valenti had already experienced the seaside city of Brighton, which he loved. In London in the Swinging Sixties, he was a waiter at the Prospect of Whitby, a famous and centuries-old tavern in the East End borough of Tower Hamlets on the banks of the River Thames. Princess Margaret was a regular, says Valenti, although he laughs looking back as much of the clientele were East End Londoners and he struggled with the slang as his command of English grew.

He learned to wait tables and then, through a friend in the French Embassy, ended up in a job in Cannes where he eventually became restaurant manager. He moved to Asia in 1978 with stints in restaurant work in both Hong Kong and Singapore before an opening came up at the Mandarin Oriental Hong Kong, which was built in 1963.

Valenti says he had never worked in hotels before. He managed the Mandarin Grill and worked in the Mandarin Oriental Bangkok. "For years there was competition between the two as to which one was the best." After being sent for training at the Savoy in London, he began the vocation to which he was best suited and to which he dedicated the major part of his working life.

"My first general manager was Andreas Hofer," says Valenti. "Tough but professional and I like that, you really learn a lot. One year at the Grill, then front office at Bangkok, then to London to learn at the Savoy."

So, who's he met, then? "I've met a lot of people," says Valenti, his face cracking into a smile. "Sarah Ferguson, she was divine. Diana was very discreet, not at all demanding. I met Richard Nixon, of course, a few years after Watergate."

On April 1, 2003, Cantopop icon and actor Leslie Cheung jumped from the 24th floor of the Mandarin to his death on the street below. To this day, his fans still remember him on that day and take flowers to that spot. While Valenti did not know him personally, he would often smile and greet him in the lobby or lift.

"He would go to the gym every single day," says Valenti. "And I had gone to the Excelsior and they called me. Mr Valenti, you must come back very quickly to the Mandarin. And it was just on the corner. First of April every year there are many flowers donated to his memory there."

As a tennis player himself, for Valenti a highlight was meeting Swedish tennis legend Bjorn Borg and playing tennis with him. "Of course he was fantastic. To me, he was an icon of tennis, the best in the world." Valenti's mother was a seamstress and his father worked on a construction site. His twin sister died due to a likely lack of nutrition in wartime Sicily. And he became an institution on the other side of the world – and one that has been recognized by the Italian government, who in the 1980s gave him the title Cavaliere Della Repubblica Italiana—the Italian knighthood.

"It's all about attitude," he says.

Learning Italian

Those who want to learn Italian attend the Hong Kong branch of the Dante Alighieri Society (DAS). It was established in 1934, the second in China, after the one in Tianjin in 1924. The study of Dante in Hong Kong and Macau had a strong tradition because the Consul General of Italy from 1899 until 1919 was Eugenio Zamboni Volpicelli (Naples 1856—Nagasaki, 1936), a polyglot, ethnologist, and historian. His mother was British, and he was very fond of Dante, translating parts of the *Divine Comedy* into Chinese.

DAS was founded in July 1889, by the Nobel Prize winner for Literature Giosuè Carducci (1835-1907), to promote Italian culture and language around the world. Today it is present in more than sixty countries. Its funding comes only from private contributors and lessons of Italian culture, arts, and language. DAS in Hong Kong was closed during the war years, but it reopened in the 1960s, thanks to the commitment of [the late] Leo Lee Tung-hai. The drive to reopen the branch here came from Giuliano Bertuccioli (1923-2001), Consul, and then Consul

General of Italy in Hong Kong and Macau from 1953 until 1960. Bertuccioli is remembered as one of the greatest Italian sinologists, with several of his books still in print.

The branch offers a variety of Italian courses ranging from Beginner I to Advanced levels. Its teachers can also teach in a company and tailor-make an approach to suit the needs of a client. In May and November, it organizes examinations of PLIDA (Progetto Lingua Italiana Dante Alighieri), the only test in Hong Kong to ascertain Italian language proficiency that is recognized by the Italian Government. Each year about 300 students attend its classes. They learn the language to work, study, or travel in Italy or have a strong personal interest in the language and culture.

Besides, to promote Italian culture and tradition, DAS works with the Consulate General of Italy in Hong Kong, the Italian Chamber of Commerce, Alessandro Manzoni School, corporate members, and other Italian cultural associations to organize Italian cultural activities, such as concerts, wine tasting, Italian outdoor lessons, and cooking classes. It offers translation services and can provide a certified and legalized translations.

In July 2014, the branch moved to a new office in Leighton Road, Causeway Bay, dedicated to the memory of Angelo Pepe, a great supporter of Italian commerce and culture in Hong Kong. The move allowed it to expand its activities significantly. The classrooms were generously sponsored by Giorgio Armani, Sugi, Generali, NRT, and Sips; Dino Capelvenere funded the library. The library has more than 3,000 Italian books and 500 DVDs for students and members of society.

CHAPTER FOUR
The Portuguese

Portuguese — Pillar of Hong Kong Society
For 150 years, the Portuguese were, after the British, the largest non-Chinese community in Hong Kong. In this chapter, we describe their long history and profile five Portuguese who reached high positions. We also describe their two main social clubs.

The Portuguese played a key role in the government, banks, professions and trading companies. They lived here for many generations. Most expatriates only stayed for the length of their assignment; when they retired, they left and returned to Britain or another country in Europe. The Portuguese, on the other hand, had their own schools, churches, social and sporting clubs and their own language. A small number rose to senior positions, such as José Pedro Braga who was the first Portuguese to serve on the Legislative Council, between 1929 and 1937 and was also chairman of the China Light and Power Company; Sir Roger Lobo, a member of the Executive Council between 1967 and 1985; and Comendador Arnaldo de Oliveira Sales, first chairman of the Urban Council between 1973 and 1981. These three were an exception. In a colony defined by class and status,

EUROPEANS IN HONG KONG

the Portuguese occupied a middle rank, between the British and other Europeans and the majority of working class Chinese below them. A glass ceiling prevented all but a small number of Portuguese from becoming chief executives or department heads, however long they had worked in a particular institution. The Portuguese in Hong Kong since the 1840s have been of mixed race. Their history goes back hundreds of years, to the early days of Portuguese trade and exploration. In the 16th Century, Portugal set up trading posts and religious missions in Goa, Malacca, Macao and Nagasaki. Male Portuguese settlers married local women, creating a mixed population with roots in India, Malaya, China and Japan. In 1639, Japan's government expelled all foreigners and sealed it off from the world. In the mid-1600s, the Dutch blockaded Goa and conquered Malacca. So Macao became Portugal's base in East Asia. The Macanese began to take shape as a cohesive community—sharing ties with Portugal, the Catholic religion, a common language and cuisine and a sense of being distinctive from the colonial Portuguese and their Chinese neighbors. They were the only people in Macao who could speak both Portuguese and Cantonese, giving them an essential intermediary role in the efficient running of the government and business.

The foundation of Hong Kong devastated the Macao economy. Just sixty-six kilometers away was the best deep-water port in south China under the laws, administration and military protection of the world's largest empire. Most foreign companies in Macao moved to the new colony to take advantage of its economic opportunities. Many Macanese made the same journey; they soon learned English. The 1853 census found 459 "Portuguese (Goa and Macao)" in Hong Kong, compared to 476 Europeans and Americans, 352 Indians, Malays and "natives of Manila" and 37,536 Chinese. Two events further accelerated this migration—the assassination of Governor Joao Maria Ferreira do Amaral by seven Chinese men in August 1849 and a major typhoon in 1874 that devastated Macao. It killed 5,000 people and destroyed 2,000 fishing boats and trading vessels. After they moved to Hong Kong, most of the Macanese lived in an area known as Mato Morro on Hong Kong Island. Located on Glenealy, Robinson Road, Caine Road and Shelley Street, they were within walking distance of the Catholic Cathedral. Many attended Mass regularly, some every day. It was a fifteen-minute walk downhill to the Central Business District where most of them worked.

The Macanese quickly found their place in the new booming city, as middlemen between the British and Chinese. Many spoke several dialects of Chinese, in addition to Cantonese and Portuguese. They served as interpreters and clerks of government departments; the Chief Clerk managed dozens of Macanese clerks below them and reported directly to their British managers. Those managers who stayed in Hong Kong for a limited period relied heavily on them. There was a similar hierarchy in the private trading firms, such as Jardine Matheson and Butterfield Swire; most of the middle managers were Portuguese. They took their place in the class system that the British established in Hong Kong as they did in other colonies. Historian Austin Coates described it in this way: "They could not rise. They were not Protestants; they were not freemasons; and they were not really Europeans. As clerks, they came and as clerks they stayed, except for a small handful of professional men who were the natural leaders of the Portuguese community." The highest post a Portuguese could achieve before World War II was Chief Clerk. Very few attended university; this involved the enormous living and study costs of going to Britain or another foreign country. The other option was Hong Kong University,

EUROPEANS IN HONG KONG

which opened in March 1912.

As the community expanded, some moved to Kowloon where housing was cheaper. Clusters of Portuguese developed in Tsim Sha Tsui, Homantin and Kowloon Tong. They had a comfortable life; most families had one domestic servant or more. The community had its own churches and social clubs, including the Club Lusitano, set up in 1866, and the Club de Recreio, set up in 1905. The members played sports including softball, cricket and hockey. Most executive positions in the government and large foreign companies were reserved for British and European expatriates. The Macanese worked for many years in these firms, but few could attain the top posts. When Shanghai boomed in the first three decades of the 20th Century, some moved there to take advantage of its new economic opportunities.

During World War II, Portugal and Macao were neutral. On December 8, 1941, the Japanese invaded Hong Kong; the British governor surrendered on Christmas Day. Most of the 10,000 Portuguese in the city fled to Macao, the place of their ancestors. It was the only place in East Asia not occupied by the Japanese. Macao Governor Gabriel Texeira generously opened the door and welcomed the refugees, including many people of Portuguese origin who had lived in Hong Kong for generations and no longer spoke the language. They were issued with identity papers which enabled them to escape. About half stayed with relatives or friends who kindly opened their homes to them. The other half stayed in refugee centers run by the Macao government and the Catholic Church. Life in Macao was difficult, with many people close to starvation; but it was better than in Hong Kong. There was a gap between the residents of Macao and the returnees. Many of them had been anglicized, spoke no Portuguese and held British nationality. Irish Jesuit priests started Colegio de Sao Luis Gonzaga in Macao, so that the young men from Hong Kong could continue their education in English.

Others stayed in Hong Kong; almost 300 Portuguese fought the Japanese alongside the Allied forces. Many served in the Hong Kong Volunteer Defense Corps; one company made its headquarters in Club Lusitano until the surrender on Christmas Day. In the battle, thirty-one Portuguese were killed and many others were interned. They worked as forced labor in squalid conditions in labor and Prisoner-of-War camps, some in Japan. In the dark years of the war, Club Lusitano became a refuge for the Portuguese community; it provided shelter and rations to many. Portugal's neutrality lent the club some protection but it was still subject to raids by the Japanese secret police, who accused members of spying for the British. Carlo Henrique Basto was arrested in 1942 during a bridge game with friends; he was convicted on the basis that the notes he wrote while playing bridge were coded messages. By September that year, he was beheaded in Stanley. In 1949, the Portuguese government bestowed the Ordem Militar de Cristo on the club in recognition of its distinguished service during the war.

The post-war period and the communist revolution of 1949 was a time of turmoil and upheaval. Some of the Portuguese in Hong Kong felt insecure of their future and emigrated to the Americas, Australia and Portugal. To dissuade his staff from leaving, Sir Arthur Morse, chief manager of the Hong Kong and Shanghai Bank, approved construction of Luso Apartments in Kowloon Tong, containing two or three bedrooms. The staff paid ten per cent of their monthly salary as rent for these apartments. A young Portuguese working for HSBC could earn HK$700-800 a month, enough to rent a two-bedroom apartment, support a wife, two children and a maid and still have money to save in the bank. In the 1950s, the main employers of Portuguese were the

EUROPEANS IN HONG KONG

government, HSBC, China Light and Power, Jardine Matheson, Butterfield & Swire and other large trading houses, as well as shipping, insurance and oil companies. For those with steady jobs, life was comfortable, with servants and many choices of leisure and cuisine. At the weekends, they went to Mass, enjoyed boating, hunting and swimming, played sports at the Club de Recreio and other venues, went to parties organized by the community to celebrate a wedding, a birthday or say farewell to someone who was leaving. Most young people married within the community, keeping it tight-knit and homogenous. After 1949, it grew with the arrival of Portuguese from Shanghai, who left after the communist revolution.

In 1947, the community ran a temporary kindergarten at Club de Recreio to meet the education needs of their children. Due to an increase in the number of students, in November 1951, the Portuguese Consul in Hong Kong, supported by the Hong Kong government and local Portuguese institutes and individuals, such as Club Lusitano, Club de Recreio, Colonel Botelho and Mr A. de O. Sales, put forward a plan to raise funds for a school mainly for local Portuguese. On June 29, 1954, the Portuguese Community Schools, Inc Escola Camões (Camões School) on 7 Cox's Road, Kowloon, was inaugurated; it was an educational milestone for the Portuguese community. Mrs Edna Chow, who started teaching there in the mid-1960s, said the premises accommodated a kindergarten and a primary school. There were 300 students. Nearly half were Portuguese and the others Eurasian, Indian, Filipino and Chinese. Besides regular subjects, like English, history, geography, hygiene and religious knowledge, the school taught Portuguese. Although the number of local Portuguese students fell in later years, the school put much effort into preserving the Portuguese cultural legacy, with Portuguese poems recited at the annual Speech Day, and emphasis on important Catholic festivals, like Christmas and Easter. In 1996, Portuguese management of the school ended and the Po Leung Kuk took over. In 1999, teachers and pupils moved to a new building at 6 Hoi Ting Road, Yau Ma Tei, under the new name. The original building in Cox's Road is now empty and locked up.

With the economic boom after the war, the Portuguese community in Hong Kong continued to grow. In 1961, the census recorded 9,388 Portuguese-speakers. But it became harder to retain the Macanese identity. While Portuguese was an official language in Macao, in Hong Kong, Cantonese and English were dominant. Many Macanese married Hong Kong partners and assimilated into the larger Cantonese-speaking community; their children did not speak Portuguese since it was not spoken at home. The language around the dinner table was likely to be Cantonese.

Many people of Portuguese descent have made their mark in the Hong Kong scene, such as Canto film star Isabella Leong, whose birth name was Luísa Isabella Nolasco da Silva. There was also Miss Hong Kong 1988 Michelle Reis, singer and show hostess Maria Cordero and Radio Television Hong Kong DJ Ray Cordeiro (郭利民), known professionally as Uncle Ray. He was born on December 12, 1924; in 2000, he was named "The World's Most Durable DJ" by the Guinness Book of Records. We have a profile of him in Chapter Eleven. There is also well-known racehorse owner Archie da Silva, famous for the exploits of his champion runner Silent Witness, the world's top sprinter for three seasons.

Things began to change after the outbreak of the Cultural Revolution in the Mainland in 1966. In 1967, it spread to Hong Kong and Macao, with riots organized by left-wing unions. Those in Hong Kong lasted for seven months and left fifty-one dead, more than 800 injured and nearly 2,000 arrested. This was a terrible shock to the Portuguese, who felt more at risk than other nationals who had a country to go back to. They believed that the left-wing militants who organized the riots wanted them and the British to leave. They felt more vulnerable to arrest or seizure of their property than the British, who had a colonial power and membership of the UN Security Council behind them. Many left for Canada, Australia, Portugal, Brazil and the United States. By the time of the handover in 1997, there were only 500 to 600 members of the Portuguese community left. Many of them had senior jobs in the law, medicine and business; their status gave them a level of protection. It would be almost impossible to find such high-ranking positions in another country.

Since the handover, economic opportunities have attracted new Portuguese to the city. They are like other expatriates and have no connection with the historic Portuguese community. They work in finance, architecture, trading, engineering, wines or run their own companies. The community today numbers about 1,000. One is Mark Valadao, a 47-year-old Luso-American who arrived in Hong Kong in 2004 to work in the finance industry. He is managing director of a private equity firm and lives with his family. "We Portuguese have a strong sense of identity," said Valadao. "We speak Portuguese together. The Portuguese are a migrant people—they have been successful, through adapting and assimilating, as well as keeping their own identity and culture. The Portuguese who were not born and raised here or in Macao see themselves as expats."

Gonçalo Frey-Ramos, 39, came to Hong Kong in 2006. He is the Asia regional manager for J Portugal Ramos Wines, as well as Ramirez, the world's oldest packer of canned seafood still in operation. He is married with three children. "Since 2009," he says, "at the request of the then General Consul (Manuel

Cansado de Carvalho), I started to organize social events for the Portuguese in Hong Kong. The first was a junk boat trip, then visits to the Club de Recreio and Club Lusitano, lunches, dinners and, of course, trying to get everyone together to watch Portugal games in the European Football Championships and World Cups.

"Since then, we also have a Facebook page "Portuguese in Hong Kong" and, more recently, we organize "Portuguese Thursdays2, a casual get-together after work," Frey-Ramos said. "On special days like June 10 — Portuguese National Day — or Christmas, we try to bring more people together. Everyone speaks Portuguese. As other nationals, we have a strong identity, so it feels good to get together. The Portuguese have a long history in Hong Kong and are connected with many of the local landmarks, the Catholic Cathedral, for example. There are roads named after the Portuguese. But most are unfamiliar with that legacy. I believe the majority of us never thought to move here permanently."

Francisco da Roza was president of the Club Lusitano, Hong Kong's oldest social club, between 2009 and 2012. He is principal coordinator of an exhibition on the Portuguese of Hong Kong, due to go on display at the Hong Kong Museum of History. He has lived in Hong Kong for more than fifty years. "We can trace our ancestors all the way back to a small village near Lisbon, but I have been here in Hong Kong for more than fifty years," he said. "My family has been in Macao for more than 300 years. Our community was more distinct than the other foreign communities (in Hong Kong). We had our churches, our schools and social and sports clubs. We were a closely knit community, with our own culture and dialect, all brought from Macao. We are part of Hong Kong. We came with the British on the founding of the new colony. The potential of the city attracted different people who came to work, to settle and make contributions. This is the foundation that made Hong Kong the international city it is today. I grew up in Macao and Hong Kong. That is why I assimilate easily with the Portuguese descendants of these two cities. During many years, the Hong Kong and Shanghai Bank had a policy of only employing Macanese. The British looked at us as acclimatized Europeans. We have been here in this part of the world for a long time and we have learned to get along with the local population. Able to speak Chinese, we were able to gain the confidence of the residents more easily."

After World War II, most of da Roza's family moved to Venezuela. He himself married a Hong Kong lady; their children have Portuguese names. "They went to international schools and attended overseas universities — and often they speak more English and Cantonese than Portuguese. Without Portuguese being spoken at home, it is hard for children to learn the language. My son can certainly swear in Portuguese. And he is a very strong supporter of the Portuguese football team," da Roza said. The exhibition at the Hong Kong Museum of History will become part of a permanent feature, "the Hong Kong Story" — that will include its foreign communities. Da Roza said that this was "a fantastic opportunity to revive the collective memory of the Hong Kong community at large." For his research, he has visited the Portuguese communities in North America and elsewhere, in search of documents, photos and other items.

In this section, we describe five prominent members of the community who attained high positions in the government, business and the law.

Jose Pedro Braga — first Portuguese member of LegCo

Jose Pedro Braga was appointed the first Portuguese member of the Legislative Council in 1929. In 1935, he was the first member of his community to become an Officer of the Order of the British Empire. He was born on August 3, 1871, in Hong Kong and educated in English at St Joseph's College, a Catholic school. At 16, he went to boarding school at St Xavier's College in Calcutta, the leading Jesuit school in India. He excelled and won a First Class pass and the only scholarship available to a European in Bengal. In May 1889, following the tragic death of three of his brothers from smallpox, he returned to Hong Kong and worked as a junior compositor in his grandfather's printing office. This prevented him from studying for the Bar, which remained a lifelong ambition he never fulfilled. He continued with the printing firm until his grandfather's death in 1900. In May 1895, he married the Australian daughter of English parents. They had thirteen children; they and his wife were devout Protestants, while he remained a Catholic. He was unable to attend the weddings of his children held in Protestant churches.

From 1902 to 1911, he was managing editor of the *Hong Kong Telegraph* and, from 1906 to 1931, Reuters correspondent in Hong Kong. In the 1930s, he became managing director of the Hong Kong Engineering and Construction Company. He was also a board member of China Light and Power. He took a great interest in public service. In 1927, he was appointed a member of the Sanitary Board. In 1929, he was became the first Portuguese member of the Legislative Council and served two full terms, until 1937. He helped to organize two Empire Trade Fairs, in 1932 and 1933, to redress a decline in commerce. Shortly after the Japanese invasion, Braga and his most members of his large family took refuge in Macao. He spent his remaining years on a book published after his death, *The Portuguese in Hongkong and China*.

His eldest son, Jack, was born in Hong Kong on May 22, 1897. During the war, he joined the British Special Operations

Executive. In Macao, he served as liaison officer between the Chinese government and British army. He organized a clandestine courier service that carried vital messages between Hong Kong, Macao, Chongqing and Allied radio stations between the Japanese lines in China.

Jose Pedro Braga died in Macao on February 14, 1944, and is buried in San Miguel Cemetery, with a bronze bust over his grave created by Italian sculptor Oseo Acconci. His example paved the way for other Portuguese to follow him into public life and LegCo. Of his thirteen children, seven emigrated, to Britain, the US, Canada and Australia. The others remained in Hong Kong. The last surviving one, Caroline, a piano teacher, died in November 1998, a year after the handover and a year before Macao reverted to Chinese sovereignty.

One of the sons who emigrated, to Australia, was Jack, who had built up over many years a library of 7,000 historical books, 500 maps and 300 paintings. Jack was a businessman, teacher, journalist and writer. His nephew Stuart Braga, a teacher and historian, said, "He had seen his father's library destroyed during World War II and only four books left. He was terrified the same thing would happen to his collection." So Jack Braga sold the library for a fire sale price of £10,000 pounds to the National Library of Australia in Canberra, which invited him to move there as a consultant. Stuart Braga was born in Hong Kong in 1939 and emigrated with his family to Australia in 1951. "During World War II, Uncle Jack knew it was a special time and collected all he could about the cultural life in Macao—musical and theater performances, church services of thanksgiving," said Stuart. "It was amazing." Asked about how the Hong Kong Portuguese should be remembered, one of those who emigrated in the 1960s said, "they should be remembered as people who share a strong communal bond, who worked hard and played well, who were good cooks and enjoyed their food, who were committed to family and, most important, who had the courage to surrender their comfortable lives to seek a better life for their families in countries where they could be fully fledged citizens."

Roger Lobo — Public Servant and Philanthropist

Another Portuguese who broke the 'glass ceiling' and joined the ruling elite was Sir Rogerio Hynsan Lobo, better known as Roger Lobo. He served in the Executive Council from 1967 to 1985. He was a businessman, public servant and philanthropist. His most famous political act, in March 1984, was to introduce a motion in the Legislative Council that called for a debate over the future of Hong Kong.

Lobo was born in Macao on September 15, 1923. At the start of the 20th Century, his father Pedro had moved to Macao from Portuguese Timor. His mother was Branca Hynsan, great-granddaughter of a Scottish colonel in the British East India Company. Pedro was a leading businessman, politician and philanthropist in Macao. Roger studied at the Lyceum in Macao and La Salle College in Hong Kong. In 1941, just before the city was about to fall to the Japanese, the Brothers assembled their Portuguese students under a tree and told them to go back to Macao before it was too late. Life there was easier than in Hong Kong, but also suffered from serious shortages. Lobo had to be inventive to find rice, fuel, electricity or a little entertainment. "I was saddened when the British and Japanese consuls had to break their friendship but was more horrified to see the Japanese consul shot by his own people for being too close to the Allies," he said. "As I looked at the body of the dead consul, I felt angry that people could just eliminate another person like that. To me, life was precious." He also flew as a pilot in Burma during the war. These experiences gave him a maturity beyond of his years. After the Japanese surrender in 1945, he joined his father's business.

In 1947, he asked his sweetheart Margaret Mary Choa to leave university in the United States and return to Hong Kong to marry him. She did; they had five sons and five daughters. He was a founding member of the Junior Chamber of Commerce and later its president.

In April 1965, he joined the Urban Council, the start of a long career in public life. From 1967 to 1985, he served on the Executive Council, first as an acting member and then a full member. He was also a member of the Legislative Council from 1972 to 1985. His most famous intervention was the "Lobo Motion" in March 1984 during the negotiations between Britain and China. No Hong Kong people were present during the negotiations; they were conducted only between British and Chinese officials. The motion demanded a full debate in LegCo before the two countries reached a final agreement on Hong Kong. He wanted to ensure that the views of Hong Kong people received the attention they deserved and were properly presented to the two governments. "The acceptability of any proposed settlement lies in whether people believe its terms will be respected and will endure," he said. "Faith cannot be created by orders. Trust cannot be induced by the exercise of power. And no settlement which fails to engender trust can possibly preserve our stability and prosperity." The motion was passed unanimously, six months before the Sino-British Joint Declaration. In local affairs, he promoted the provision of mobile and floating libraries, control of hawkers and the home ownership scheme, to provide affordable housing to the middle class.

He was also chairman of the Hong Kong Broadcasting Authority from 1989 to 1997. He joined the Civil Aid Services and served as its commissioner from 1977 until 1993. He also served on the Advisory Committee on Corruption, Tenancy Tribunal and the Medical Development Advisory Committee. In 1972, he received the Order of the British Empire and, in 1978, the Commander of the British Empire. He was knighted in 1984.

He was active in philanthropy, working with the Society for the Deaf, Society for the Blind, Caritas Committee and Community Chest. The Pope gave him the Honor of Commander of the Order of St Gregory for his work with Caritas and service to the community.

He died on April 18, 2015, at the age of ninety-one. On July 11, Cardinal John Tong Hon held a memorial Mass in his honor at a packed Cathedral of the Immaculate Conception. To describe Lobo's life, son-in-law Kenneth Morrison quoted from the prophet Micah, "And what does the Lord require of you? To act justly, to love mercy and walk humbly with your God." Son Pedro Jose Lobo said, "We know our dad as someone who had a profound sense of helping others in need. He was always asking what he could do to help and reached out to many. We never knew growing up how many lives he had truly touched. He was a humble man who never spoke of some aspects of his achievements. He was an accomplished athlete in many sports, he was a sprinter, a calligrapher and interior designer."

Arnaldo de Oliviera Sales — Father of Hong Kong Sport

Commendador Arnaldo de Oliviera Sales was President of the Amateur Sports Federation and Olympic Committee of Hong Kong from 1967 to 1998. He was the most important sports administrator in the city for half a century. It was his drive and connections that enabled Hong Kong to compete in the Olympics as a separate entity after 1997. He was also Chairman of the Urban Council from 1973 to 1983.

Sales was born on January 13, 1920, into a Portuguese family in Shamian (沙面), a foreign concession in Guangzhou, where his family had a business. At the age of eight, he moved to Hong Kong and attended Catholic schools, including La Salle College. He also studied at St Joseph's Seminary in Macao. After attending business school, he returned to Hong Kong to join the family business. During World War II, he took refuge in Macao, like many Portuguese in Hong Kong. He married Edith Nolasco da Silva, a member of one of the wealthiest Macanese families; they had no children.

In 1950, he and like-minded people founded the Amateur Sports Federation and Olympic Committee (ASFOC) and later became its president. In 1951, it was formally recognized as a member of the International Olympic Committee (IOC) and, in 1952, the Olympic Council of Asia. On March 8, 1999, it was formally renamed the Sports Federation & Olympic Committee of Hong Kong China. Today it has seventy-nine member associations.

Sales joined the Junior Chamber of Commerce; in 1955, he was elected its world president and visited more than eighty countries in that role. In April 1957, he was appointed a member of the Urban Council and became chairman in April 1973, a position he held until 1981. While it had limited power in a system tightly controlled by the colonial government, Sales used those powers to the full. The Urban Council built playing fields, concert halls, public parks and swimming pools that are widely used today. He was an efficient administrator, with a stern, abrasive personality that upset people, including Governors. This got things done but was probably the reason he was never appointed to the Legislative or Executive Councils. He was a member of the Hong Kong Basic Law Consultative Committee.

One of his great achievements was to obtain recognition for the Hong Kong team at international sporting events after 1997.

The team competed as "China, Hong Kong". He was chief of mission of Hong Kong at all the Olympic Games from 1952 to 1988 and to the Asian and Commonwealth Games from 1958 to 1990. He was delegate and spokesman of several Olympic Committees. He sternly opposed professionalism and insisted the Olympics should be only amateur. He maintained this opposition even after many professional athletes competed in the Games, in basketball, cycling, tennis and golf, from the 1980s onwards.

He was president of the Club de Recreio from 1960 to 2012 and long-serving president of the Club Lusitano. He was also the longest serving chairman and honorary life president of the Victoria Recreation Club (VRC). The VRC is Hong Kong's oldest private club; it opened in 1849 on the shoreline of Victoria Hall where the City Hall stands today. The early meetings of the ASFOC were held in its clubhouse in Central. Now the club is based in spacious grounds in Sai Kung. Sales was also active in philanthropy; he was charity President of the Hong Kong Society for the Blind. He received honors from the governments of Britain, Portugal, Spain, Italy, Japan and Brazil. He retained his Portuguese nationality throughout his life.

His finest hour came during the Munich Olympics Games in September 1972. Palestinian gunmen had taken over the building where the Israeli athletes were staying. The Hong Kong team was housed in the same block. Three of the team escaped by climbing on the roof — but two others, the judo and swimming coaches, were trapped inside. With the deadline set by the gunmen approaching, Sales insisted on going inside the building to try to rescue the remaining two. He met the leader of the Black September group and asked for their release. The two walked to the rooms where the two coaches were staying. One was in his underwear; Sales told him to put on his trousers quickly. He then escorted the two out of the building to safety. "When I walked out with them, I heard a great cheer," Sales said later. "It never occurred to me that I might be in danger. My mind was focused on getting the Hong Kong athletes out. It was very sad that it ended in a tragedy." The Palestinians killed eleven Israeli athletes and one German police officer. All the members of the terrorist group were eventually killed.

Sales died on March 6, 2020, at the age of 100, at the Hong Kong Sanatorium and Hospital. More than 200 people attended a Funeral Mass at St Joseph's Church on March 27 and he was buried at St Michael's Cemetery in Happy Valley.

The SFOC issued a statement after his death: "Being one of the founders of the federation, Mr Sales devoted more than half a century as honorary secretary general, chairman, president and honorary life president ... Under his presidency from 1967 to 1998, Hong Kong athletes gradually gained recognition in many international multi-sports games such as the Commonwealth Games, Olympic Games and Asian Games. With his vision and utmost effort, Hong Kong was retained as a separate sporting entity after the changeover of sovereignty, which greatly supported the continuum of worldwide exposure of Hong Kong athletes for sports competitions beyond 1997." Timothy Fok Tsunting, who succeeded him as President of the Federation, said, "Sales always believed sports can fulfill a person's happiness at a time when sport was still a luxury in Hong Kong society."

Leonardo e Castro – Leading Lawyer and Legislator

Leonardo Horacio d'Almada e Castro Jnr was one of the few Portuguese to break the 'glass ceiling'. He was the first local Portuguese barrister in Hong Kong and served twenty-two years on the Legislative and Executive Councils. After World War II, he served as the President of the General Military Court that tried Japanese war criminals. He played an important role in the official and social life of Hong Kong for forty years. He was a leader of the Portuguese community.

He was born on May 28, 1904, in Hong Kong, the son of a prominent solicitor. He was educated at St Joseph's College, Hong Kong University and Exeter College, Oxford, where he read jurisprudence. A member of the Middle Temple, he was called to the English bar in 1926 and returned to Hong Kong in 1927. He began a successful career as a barrister. In 1933, he married Clotilde Belmira Barretto, who was appointed Hong Kong's first female Justice of the Peace in 1947. Their marriage lasted sixty-two years. In 1933, he became president of the Kowloon Residents' Association, his first step into public life. In February 1937, he was appointed to the Legislative Council, succeeding J.P. Braga at the young age of thirty-three. After the war, he resumed membership, until 1953. From 1949 to 1959, he was a member of the Executive Council, the first Portuguese to hold this post; he retired as Senior Unofficial Member. He served on the two Councils for twenty-two years.

During the Japanese invasion, he served as a warden in the Air Raid Precautions Service in Wong Nei Chung Road Hong Kong Island. In early 1942, after a visit to Macao, he was interrogated by the Japanese military police on suspicion of spying for the British; he was held for a few days and then released. Because of this experience, he decided to resettle in Macao. There he served as Liaison Officer between the British and Portuguese in assisting the thousands of refugees. In June 1945, the British Army Aid Group secreted him and his wife out of Macao to join the Hong Kong Planning Unit in London; this involved a dangerous twenty-four-day journey over 250 miles across enemy-held territory. They traveled by foot, sampan, bicycle, riverboat and sedan chair. He and his wife were flown from Kunming to

India and then London. After Japan's surrender in August 1945, he returned at once to Hong Kong. He served as the de facto Chief Justice under the British military administration; it was an interim justice trying robberies and other cases. On May 1, 1946, the new Supreme Court was re-constituted, with the arrival of Chief Justice Sir Henry Blackall, e Castro returned to private practise. He and Blackall never sat at the same time. In 1947, he became the first Hong Kong Portuguese King's Counsel.

In 1949, the Portuguese government honored him with the Ordem de Cristo for his service to the Portuguese community in Hong Kong. In 1953, he received the honor of the Commander of the Most Excellent Order of the British Empire. He was chairman of the Hong Kong Bar Association on six occasions. In 1968, he and his wife retired to a home near Cascais, a coastal town near Lisbon. He continued to take briefs in Hong Kong and regularly returned here. He died on September 4, 1996, in Cascais, aged 92.

Roberto Ribeiro — Judge of Court of Final Appeal

Roberto Alexandre Vieira Ribeiro (李義) who has held the highest position in the legal system of Hong Kong. In September 2000, he was appointed a Permanent Judge of the Court of Final Appeal, a post he holds today. He is one of three permanent judges of the court and the longest-serving.

He was born on March 20, 1949. in Hong Kong into a family of Portuguese descent. He studied at La Salle College in Hong Kong and went on to read law at the London School of Economics. There he obtained his LLB in 1971 and LLM in 1972. On returning to Hong Kong, he taught as a Lecturer in Law at the University of Hong Kong from 1972 to 1979. His subjects included criminal law, jurisprudence, labor law and civil procedure.

He was called to the English Bar at the Inner Temple and to the Hong Kong Bar in 1978 and entered full-time private practise in

Hong Kong in 1979, focusing generally in the field of commercial law. In 1990, he was appointed Queen's Counsel.

In 1997, he was appointed Recorder of the Court of First Instance. In 1999, he joined the Judiciary as a Judge of the Court of First Instance. In January 2000, he was appointed a Justice of Appeal and, in September of that year, appointed a Permanent Judge of the Court of Final Appeal. This is the final appellate court within the court system of the Hong Kong SAR. It plays an important part in the development of the common law in the city. It was established on July 1, 1997, and replaced the Judicial Committee of the Privy Council in London as the highest appellate court in Hong Kong after the handover.

Justice Ribeiro was the Vice-Chairman of the Chief Justice's Working Party on Civil Justice Reform and drafted the Interim and Final Reports on which the procedural reforms adopted in 2009 were based. From 2008 to 2014, he was a member of the Judicial Officers Recommendation Commission that recommends judicial appointments. He presently (2019) chairs the Judiciary's Committee on Information Technology.

Mr Justice Ribeiro is an Honorary Bencher of the Inner Temple, an Honorary Fellow of the London School of Economics and an Honorary Fellow of St Hugh's College, Oxford. In 2019, he was admitted to the degree of Doctor of Laws (honoris causa) by the University of Hong Kong.

Club de Lusitano

The Portuguese set up two social clubs. The first was the Club Lusitano founded on December 17, 1866, as a center for Portuguese social life. It derives its name from the ancient Iberian Roman Province of Lusitania. Today it is on the twenty-third floor of a club-owned building on Ice House Street in Central. The condition of membership is Portuguese heritage.

The first club house was financed in large part by Joao Antonio Baretto and Delfino Noronha, two prominent members of the community. They covered three-quarters of the construction costs for a large property on Shelley Street in the Mid-Levels district. It was a neighborhood that was home to many Portuguese who had moved from Macao. The club only admitted men as members; it served as a center for culture and community. It included a large reception room and library, several meeting rooms and a theater — the venue for all performers in the colony before the City Hall Theater opened in 1869. The balls, theater performances and official ceremonies hosted by the club contributed greatly to the integration of the Portuguese community into the British colony. Another factor was the generosity of the small community, which largely funded the club and made significant contributions to establishing the early Catholic institutions in the city, from the Canossian Mission, founded in 1860, to the Cathedral of the Immaculate Conception, completed in 1888.

The Lusitano Challenge Cup, an annual horse race organized by Club Lusitano (CL), is even older than the club itself. Then called the Lusitano Cup, the inaugural race was held at Happy Valley racecourse in 1863, and renamed in 1866, the year of the club's founding. Still held today, this Class 3 race covers 1,400 meters on the track at the Sha Tin racecourse with HK$1 million prize money.

On 17 December 17, 1920, exactly fifty-four years after completing the original club, the members laid the foundation stone of a new site at 16 Ice House Street, where the club still operates today. The property was purchased by a member, AML Soares, who then sold it to the club at cost. The governors of Hong Kong and Macao attended the opening ceremony — which was unsurprising, given that governors, military personnel and overseas delegations had frequented the club for decades. The club maintained strict rules on dress and members' conduct; it developed a reputation for its high standard of billiards, bridge and other card games. In March 1925, A.J. Osmond, the then billiard champion of Hong Kong, hit a break of 267 at the club. Nearly a century later, the record still stands.

The most famous member of the club during this era was José Pedro Braga. The grandson of founding member Delfino Noronha, Braga began his career in his grandfather's printing press. He served as managing director of the *Hong Kong Telegraph* and spent decades as a Reuters' correspondent in the colony before leaving journalism. A successful businessman, he worked closely with the Kadoorie family; in 1929, he became the first Portuguese appointed to the Legislative Council where he served until 1937.

In 1964, the club demolished their building on Ice House Street and replaced it with a 12-story structure designed by Macanese architect Alfredo V. Alvares. Club Lusitano occupied the top five floors—more than 1,000 square meters. It leased the lower floors to the Philippines-based Equitable Bank; subsequent tenants included the Hong Kong government and Hong Kong Shanghai Banking Corporation. Rents provided 95 percent of the club's income, enabling it to keep down costs and membership fees.

In 1996, the club building was demolished and replaced with a twenty-7story highrise, designed by Macanese architect Comendador Gustavo da Roza and completed in 2002. Below the five top floors occupied by the club are twenty floors of office space and a threelevel ground floor retail podium. A threestory Cruz de Cristo sits on top of the building; it recalls the early Portuguese ships which carried the distinctive, equalarmed red cross as a symbol of their faith. The five floors include a restaurant, bar and lounge, pastelaria, library, an office, ballroom, and other function rooms.

The grand ballroom, on the 27th floor, is the Salao de Nobre Camoes. It is the most spectacular room in the club. Two walls of floor-to-ceiling windows afford spectacular views of the shining skyscrapers of Hong Kong. They overlook the home and office of the Chief Executive on one side and the HSBC building on the other. One wall displays two stanzas from the epic work Os Lusíadas by Luís Vaz de Camões, for whom the room is named. The other features a map of the world at the entrance showing the routes taken by pioneering Portuguese explorers and mariners. In 2003, the club admitted women members for the first time.

Today the club has about 500 members, of whom 320 are active; the rest do not live in Hong Kong. The Club president since 2014 is Patrick Antonio de Lemos Rozario, an accountant by training. The club hosts many annual events, from festivities for Portuguese National Day and Fésta de São João in June, to a newly created, black-tie End of Year Gala Ball and a Christmas lunch in December. They invite celebrity chefs for special dinners, organize film screenings and talks, and host music and reading events. The club's membership reflects the Portuguese diaspora, with members from Australia, China, Canada, India, Brazil, the US and UK, as well as Portugal. To join, a person must provide proof of Portuguese ancestry or nationality. Acquiring such proof is greatly helped by neighboring Macao. "Macao never had a major conflict, so its records, including its church documents, are intact," said Rozario. "There are also shipping records that show the arrival of ships from Portugal. People often use these to prove their lineage." Despite their shared Portuguese heritage, most members do not speak the language. The primary language in the club is English; many members also speak Cantonese.

Rozario himself is Macanese. "My first Portuguese ancestors arrived in Macao in the 1750s, inter-marrying with different nationalities and later arrivals from Portugal," he said. "I grew up in Hong Kong and remember going to Macao for christenings, weddings, and birthday parties." As a teenager, he left for education in Canada and became an accountant. He worked in Canada and the US before returning to Hong Kong in 1996. "I wanted to see the handover," he said. "My parents and brother live in Toronto. I rejoined the club and have many schoolmates here." Many like him have returned to Hong Kong since the handover, as well as young people from Portugal and Brazil, in search of economic opportunities. "In seeking new members, we are reaching out to these people," he said. "In the past, we did not have to try very hard. Everyone from Hong Kong knew each other." His story echoes the odyssey of many members of the city's Portuguese community since the 1960s; instability, violence and limited opportunity spurred mass immigration to English- and Portuguese-speaking countries. Now many are returning; they are breathing new life into a club so central to the history of Portuguese in Hong Kong.

In 2019, Club Lusitano has completely renovated the premises to reflect its culture and heritage and provide a modern facility for members to enjoy and carry out their business, social and family activities. Club Lusitano serves mainly Portuguese produce and Rozario is certain that Club Lusitano has the largest collection of Portuguese wines and spirits outside of Portugal.

Club de Recreio
The Club de Recreio (Recreation), on Gascoigne Road, was the second club in Hong Kong established for Portuguese people, after the Club Lusitano. It was set up in 1906 and has been ever since one of the leading clubs in the city in soccer, hockey, cricket and other sports. It was an ideal location for the many Portuguese families who lived in Kowloon Tong, Homantin, Tsim Sha Tsui and other areas of Kowloon. In addition, it had outdoor space to

play sports, which CL did not. So the CL became a gentleman's club, suitable for business lunches and dinners and formal events hosting visiting dignitaries from the Hong Kong and Macao governments and abroad. The Club de Recreio attracted younger people and families who wanted sports and entertainment after work and at the weekends. It had the larger membership of the two clubs, peaking at more than 300 in the 1950s and 1960s.

From its inception, it organized athletic events and competitions, for cricket, field hockey, soccer, lawn bowls, tennis and badminton. It also offered billiards and snooker, cards, mahjong and tombola—similar to bingo. It had a men's-only bar and dining room. Its most famous sporting family was the Gasano family whose seven sons, out of nine children, excelled. They were a second-generation Portuguese family born in Hong Kong. The sons shone at soccer, cricket, rowing and other sports. Club de Recreio was one of the most important social and sporting centers for the Portuguese in the city.

After the emigration of the community from the 1960s, the membership of both the CL and the Club de Recreio declined. Both relaxed the rules for entry, admitting members from other communities. Today the majority of members of the Club de Recreio are Chinese.

Broadcasting King

Reinaldo Maria Cordeiro, better known as Uncle Ray, was a Hong Kong institution, beloved by many in the community. In May 2020, he retired at the age of 96 after more than seventy years in broadcasting. He died peacefully on January 13, 2023, aged 98, in a Hong Kong hospital, surrounded by his closest friends.

With his trademark cap, glasses and beard, he was instantly recognizable; his voice had been a part of the airwaves for such a long time that it feels odd that he will no longer be that late-night anchor man. In 2000, he was recognized by Guinness World Records as the 'World's Most Durable DJ', although he was surpassed by a DJ in America by a few months in terms of longevity on the mic.

In 1924, Cordeiro was born into a large Hong Kong Portuguese family. He grew up in Wan Chai and attended St Joseph's College; his education was interrupted when the Japanese military invaded Hong Kong in December 1941. He and his family headed to Macao, which, as a Portuguese territory, was neutral. However, there were food shortages and life was far from easy.

The Portuguese community from Hong Kong rallied together as refugees. Cordeiro recalled a Christmas and New Year's ball that was organized during that time when a band was hired and it was an opportunity for people to listen to music, dance and forget their troubles.

It was there as a teenager that Uncle Ray really discovered his love of music. Cordeiro happily watched the drummer and knew that was the instrument that he wanted to learn. He already loved drummers, such as Gene Krupa (who played with Benny Goodman) and Buddy Rich, so he decided to learn himself.

Post-war, Cordeiro joined a few of his Portuguese friends in becoming a prison warden at Stanley Prison for a year. He would later work at HSBC for four years as a bank clerk. His father already worked there, but the work bored Ray. His solace was to perform with "Ray and the Band" in the evenings. He would later perform with his brother, Armando on the played saxophone and with other musicians, they would get gigs at the Club de Recreio, Club Lusitano and other clubs around Hong Kong.

In 1949, Armando, who worked as a scriptwriter at Radio Rediffusion, would be instrumental in changing the course of Cordeiro's life. He told his younger brother that there was another scriptwriter job going. Uncle Ray was there for eleven years but soon moved behind the microphone and his first program was *Progressive Jazz*, which showcased the kind of music his own band was playing at that time. He also fronted two live shows *Talent Quest* and *Rumpus Time*, with big band leaders such as Tony Carpio and other later famous names competing on the show.

Then came *The Beginners Please* in 1951, which was the first time the world heard a young British soldier stationed here — Terence Edward Parsons, who later would become famous as Matt Monro.

In 1960, Cordeiro left Rediffusion and joined Radio Hong Kong as Head of Light Music. With him came a little bit of modernity for this staid government station. He would inject a bit of life with several live music shows, in a studio, with live bands. These included *Lucky Dip*, a show for teenagers, who would write down their requests and put them in a barrel, ready to be picked out.

Meanwhile, local live bands such as Teddy Robin and the Playboys, and singers such as Christine Samson, would have a chance to perform both live on radio and before a studio audience.

One of Uncle Ray's favorite stories was how, in 1964, he was sent to London for three months on a BBC course. It was a chance to improve his studio technical capabilities and broadcasting skills. At the end of the course, he had two weeks before he was due to fly back to Hong Kong; he wanted to use the opportunity to do interviews with bands in London that he could take back for Hong Kong listeners.

He headed to EMI, and, by a marvellous stroke of serendipity, the Beatles were having a press conference the following day. Then there was another press conference with the Beatles for foreign correspondents later in the week—so Cordeiro went to that. This happened to be ahead of an Asia tour where the Fab Four were due to come to Hong Kong. Due to ill health, Ringo Starr would not make it to Hong Kong that year and was replaced by drummer Jimmie Nicole, but Cordeiro talked to three Beatles at Kai Tak Airport. So that was three interviews with the Beatles in one week!

Over the decades, it is no exaggeration to say that Cordeiro knew anybody and everybody in the music scene both locally and the international stars who came through. He did not meet Elvis, but there are not many others he hadn't met. He was good friends with Cliff Richard, and there is a fun photograph that Cordeiro has of him interviewing a touring—and perhaps a bit tired—Elton John, who is lying on a sofa in his hotel suite. Cordeiro asked him where he would like to do the interview, and he answered, "How about here?"

Locally, Cordeiro helped promote the careers of many local singers from the 60s onwards, including Maria Cordero, Christine Samson and others. He knew singer Mona Fong well, although she was already an established singer when he met her. They would remain lifelong friends.

In 1970, Cordeiro launched *All The Way with Ray*, a four-hour program on weekday nights at RTHK, where the first half was pop numbers usually targeted at an older audience –Cliff Richard, Frank Sinatra, etc—and the second half going into the early hours after midnight would be nostalgia. As Canto pop took over the airwaves, so the bands that had sung in English disappeared. Throughout this time and over the coming decades, Cordeiro was meeting and interviewing stars as they come into Hong Kong for concerts.

In 1987, Cordeiro was awarded an MBE and ten years later received a lifetime achievement award from RTHK. In 2000, he was recognized by Guinness World Records as the 'World's Most Durable DJ, in 2008 he received a Bronze Bauhinia and in 2012 was named an honorary fellow of the Academy for Performing Arts.

In May, 2020, after a five-month hiatus due to the Covid-19 pandemic, Cordeiro returned to the studio for one final week of *All the Way with Ray*. After heart surgery a decade earlier, four hours became three, a program that he has kept going for more than fifty years, and one where any number of Hong Kong taxi drivers have learned their English listening to him on their nightshifts.

At the same time, he published his autobiography — also called *All the Way with Ray* — which describes his love of music and bringing it to his listenership from behind the microphone — for more than 70 years.

CHAPTER FIVE
The Spanish

This chapter describes the Spanish presence in Hong Kong. Its colonial empire was in Central and South America; that is where its people went to make a new life. The only Spanish colony in Asia was the Philippines; it ceded the country to the United States after its defeat in the Spanish-American War in 1898.

As a result, the Spanish presence in Hong Kong has been limited, numbering about 400 in the 1990s and rising to 2,000 today, with major Spanish companies opening offices here and the arrival of professionals in finance and other firms. Historically, Spanish emigrants went to the Americas, not Asia. Major Spanish firms operating here include Banco Bilbao Vizcaya Argentaria (BBVA), Telefonica and Santander. Most of the community are business people, especially in finance, and their families. Another substantial group are young Spaniards working as chefs in the city's restaurants, or in the food and beverage sector; Spanish foods and wines are getting extremely popular. One important aspect of local culture that attracts Spaniards is the value Chinese attach to family life, as they do. Both come together around food; the culinary culture is a common bond in Chinese and in Spanish culture. The Spanish residents appreciate the city's vibrant cosmopolitism and good environment for families with small children: excellent international schools: the natural landscape, the mountains and the sea, as Spanish enjoy activities outdoors, especially sports. For example, the Spanish teams are successful in the annual Dragon Boat races.

Formerly known as the Spanish Business Association, the Spanish Chamber of Commerce was founded in 1991 by a group of Spanish entrepreneurs. Today it has more than 120 members, including corporate, individual and overseas members and non-profits. It organizes more than fifty events a year. One prominent Spaniard in Hong Kong is Juan Dedeu, President of the China Consultants Group; he is or has been a member of the Boards of Directors of nine companies with mixed investment in the PRC. A delegate of the Barcelona Port Authority (BPA) in China, he was a founding member of the Spanish Business Association in Hong Kong (1990) and founding member of the European Chamber of Commerce in Hong Kong (1994). He was President of the Spanish Business Association in Hong Kong from 1992 to 1995) and President of the Official Spanish Chamber of Commerce in Hong Kong from 2000 to 2002. He opened the office of the BPA in Hong Kong on August 8, 1988, an auspicious date for the Chinese with four eights in it. Connected with 209 ports around the world, Barcelona is one of the largest commercial and industrial center in the Mediterranean; it moves 3.5 million full containers each year, of which 23 percent came from or went to China. In 2018, the port handled a record traffic of sixty-seven million tons, up ten percent on a year earlier. "Hong Kong is and will continue to be the main driver of the Port of Barcelona's business with the Greater Bay Area (GBA)," he said in an interview in February 2020. "We believe that, with its long history of being the gateway to China, its experience and expertise as a financial center and its historic connections to the international community, can play a key role in making the (GBA) initiative a success ... The city has to look forward and take on board the reality that it is an integral part of China and fully immerse itself in big projects such as the GBA initiative, to ensure future prosperity and success."

Spain's greatest contribution to the city has been its priests. In 1842, the first Catholic Mass in Hong Kong was celebrated by a Spanish priest for Irish soldiers of the British army garrison. In 1861, the Dominicans established a Procuration House in Caine Road, the start of a presence that has lasted more than 150 years.

"The 19th Century was the worst century for Spain," said Juan José Morales, an entrepreneur and historian who has lived in Hong Kong since 1996. "The country was crippled by the loss of a vast empire, ravaged by several civil wars, revolutions, military coups and struggles for dynastic succession. It has a harsh geography and is the most mountainous country in Europe, after Switzerland. It was sparsely populated. During that century, when Spanish people emigrated, they went to South and Central America where they shared the Spanish language. They did not come to Asia, it was too difficult. Similarly, the natural market for Spanish companies was the Americas, not East Asia. The Spanish population in the Philippines was always limited, 5,000 at maximum, most of them priests. The year 1898 was called 'El Desastre' — we lost the last remains of the empire, the Philippines and the Mariana islands in the Pacific, and we lost Cuba and Puerto Rico in America."

Mexican Dollar

With the Portuguese, the Spanish were the first Europeans to reach Asia. A Spanish expedition led by Magellan (1519-1522) was the first to cross the Pacific. After the Portuguese captain died in the Philippines, Juan Sebastián de Elcano managed to lead the only remaining vessel, Nao Victoria, back to Spain, becoming the first to circumnavigate the world. But it was not until 1565 that an expedition led by Andrés de Urdaneta managed to find a route eastwards across the Pacific, from the Philippines to Mexico or New Spain. Previously, the complexities of weather, winds and currents had prevented this achievement. This meant European ships could cross the Pacific in both directions for the first time. In 1571, the Spanish established Manila as the capital of their new territory, the Philippines. In 1573, the first galleon left Manila for Mexico laden with Chinese goods, mainly silk. This China trade developed rapidly; by 1587, a single cargo could be worth as much as two million pesos. By 1602, about 30,000 Chinese lived in Manila. Over 250 years from 1573, there were 400 sailings of the Manila galleon; a single shipment could set up a merchant for his whole life. From Acapulco, the goods were taken to the Caribbean port of Veracruz, from where vessels took them to Seville, in Spain, and the markets of Europe. With the Portuguese, the Spanish were pioneers of the China trade. The era of the Manila galleon ended in 1815 with the Mexican War of Independence. But the most important article of trade was silver, not silk, for silver from the mines in Spanish America was to become the first international currency. China was the most populous country on earth and needed vast amounts of silver to run its growing economy; it was becoming the first factory of the world. Soon the Spanish silver coin was the first global currency.

The Spanish were the only Europeans to navigate the Pacific for more than two centuries; hence, this vast ocean was called *The Spanish Lake*, a book by Australian historian Oskar H.K. Spate. But in 1743, the capture of the Spanish Galleon *Nuestra Señora de Covadonga* in Philippines waters by British Commodore George Anson was to change history. With a rich cargo of silver, Anson not only gained a massive booty for himself and his family, shared with the British crown; he also took the Spanish secret maps that were immediately published and would allow other countries to navigate the Pacific more safely. Anson's Pacific expedition was a disaster otherwise, with only 188 men of the original 1,854 surviving. It was during this expedition that, on their way to Macao and Guangzhou, the British first spotted Hong Kong.

An important contribution to Hong Kong and the rest of Asia was the Spanish silver coin, Real de a ocho, which became the main currency of the world. It was later called the Mexican dollar, because it was mainly minted in Mexico. It developed because China had little interest in outside goods but would accept silver. During much of the 19th Century, it was one of the most widely accepted currencies in Hong Kong, popular with residents and merchants. In 1866, the Hong Kong government created a mint (香港造幣廠) to provide a steady supply of silver dollars in the city. But the coins were not well received; in 1868, the site was sold to Jardine Matheson and the equipment sold to the new Japanese Mint in Osaka.

In the 1920s, a Spanish architect, Abelardo Lafuente, based in Shanghai, designed interiors for the Hong Kong Hotel and Repulse Bay Hotel, and for the Peninsula Hotel in 1926.

Father Francisco

Father Francisco de las Heras Miguel has served the people of Hong Kong for more than fifty years since his arrival in February 1972, on the third day of the New Year of the Rat. Since 1976, he has worked at Rosaryhill, a Catholic school (玫瑰崗學校) established by the Dominican Order in September 1959 on Stubbs Road in the Mid-Levels. He was Principal of the Primary School from 1983 to 1990 and Principal of the Secondary School from 1993 to 2006. He was the school Supervisor from 1993 to 1999 and from 2005 to 2013. Since 2013, he has been coordinator of its Spanish language programs. He lives with his fellow priests in residential quarters on the sixth floor of the school. Today it has 1,700 students in kindergarten, primary and secondary; in the first two sections, ninety per cent of the students are Chinese and, in the secondary school, half Chinese and half from Europe, South and Southeast Asia. It uses both English and Cantonese as a medium of instruction. "I have always felt comfortable here. I was impressed by the willingness of Hong Kong people to support foreigners," he said in an interview. "They listen to you and make you and your ideas better. I felt rewarded. I was also made welcome by the other Dominican Fathers here. They were very supportive."

Father Francisco was born on April 2, 1946, in a small village in La Horra in Burgos Province in northern Spain. His was a very traditional Catholic family, well established in the area. His father was a farmer and he had nine brothers and sisters. After attending the local primary school, the young Francisco decided at the age of nine to enter a Dominican seminary. He passed the entrance exam and, despite the misgivings of his parents to lose their son so young, he left home at the age of nine and a half. "I took a train for the first time in my life. On one day, I took two trains and then a taxi and arrived in the evening." His destination was a school in Olmedo in central Spain; it prepared boys who wanted to become priests. His superior there, a missionary in China for many years, told the students about the country. There Francisco also learned of China from Monsignor Teodoro Labrador, who had been the last Bishop of Fuzhou before 1949; he had served one year in prison before being expelled to Hong Kong and returning to Spain. Two brothers also attended a seminary, learning philosophy but decided not to become priests. Only Francisco went ahead, saying, "It is difficult to say how you find the call."

In 1961, aged 15, he joined the Dominican order and received the habit. For the next nine years, he studied philosophy and theology in Madrid and Avila. He became involved in social action, as one of several student-brothers helping 150-200 children who lived in shanty towns around Madrid; they organized lessons and activities after school. This interest in working with young people persuaded his superiors to send him to work in the school in Hong Kong. "I had no idea of Hong Kong then. I knew more of Japan and the Philippines. One of my superiors said that, since I liked children, I should go to Hong Kong where the order had a school." So, for three months, he went once or twice a week to the British Council in Madrid to improve his poor English. On the third day of the Rat in 1972, he found himself in this strange place on the other side of the world. On June 21 that year, he was ordained as a priest in Hong Kong, the first ordination in the Rosaryhill School Chapel, by Dominican Bishop Monsignor Juan Bautista Velasco.

He started with private lessons every day to learn English better. Then, in 1973, he started studying Cantonese. In the summer, he enrolled for a two-year course at New Asia College at Chinese University; it was popular with foreign priests, nuns and ministers to learn the language. At the same time, he worked at Rosaryhill School, teaching Spanish and helping with administration and training. It had 5,500 students, with an average of forty-two per class, in kindergarten, primary and secondary. From 1960, it had offered Mandarin as a third language, one of the few schools in Hong Kong to do so at that time. From 1976 to 1978, Francisco studied in the United Kingdom, to improve his English and earn a Diploma of Advanced Studies in Education.

At Rosaryhill, he has taught Spanish, Religious Knowledge and Social Ethics. "It was challenging for me," he said. "There was no reaction, no response and no complaints from the students. That is the normal pattern of students in Hong Kong. They do not put their thoughts into words, perhaps out of fear of being laughed at by others. Even in Cantonese, they do not wish to speak. Nowadays, with the use of media in the classroom, there is more response. From ten years ago, we have had an influx of Southeast Asian students, including Filipinos; they talk a lot. This was a big problem for the teachers who felt interrupted and were not comfortable. There were disciplinary issues. Now the teachers are more used to this and classes are more active." Today the school has 1,700 students, with 700 in the kindergarten, 650 in primary and 400 in secondary. Of the first two, 90 percent of students are Chinese. In secondary, half are Chinese and half from overseas, mostly Filipinos, Indians, Pakistanis and Nepalis. In 2023, the school's sponsoring body, the Dominican Missions announced that the secondary school would cease operations from the 2025-26 academic year because of a fall in enrolments and financial difficulties. It said it would combine its kindergarten and primary school with Dalton School Hong Kong. The school supervisor, Hyacinth He, said that it was increasingly difficult to maintain high-quality education within a limited budget.

Father Francisco has served for fifty years in Hong Kong. Throughout his years here, he has retained close relations with his family. "When I left Spain, one of my brothers told me to write letters regularly to our parents. As a form of relaxation after work, I wrote them three letters every two weeks. Sometimes there was not enough to fill up the page, so I would invent small incidents. The letters were 80 percent positive; if I felt sick or depressed, I did not speak of it. My father retired and moved to Madrid; he also wrote regularly and was creative, too.

"Now I am 74 and semi-retired. I could request my superior

to go to Spain. I could retire and live in one of our Dominican houses there. My six brothers and sisters live in Madrid and would like me to help look after my mother, who is 102. But I do not wish to retire now. I have good relations with the parents, students and old boys of the school. Although it is better to go back when you can still help. An old man is not an asset but a burden."

Rosaryhill School was established in September 1959, when it took over the Dominican Monastery of St Albert the Great. Its founder was Father Eutimio Gonzalez, the Procurator of the Dominican Missions in Asia. His statue stands outside the main entrance. It is situated in the Mid-Levels, an expensive residential area on Hong Kong Island, far from where most students lived. So, in 1959, the school set up a department of transport to arrange buses for them; today it has a fleet of eighteen. It started with 197 children in the kindergarten and 205 pupils in the primary school. The site could not meet the requirements of a modern school, so the Order commissioned construction of an eight-story building. It opened in 1963 with 520 children in the kindergarten and 1,775 at the primary level. It was an English-language medium school, with two years of kindergarten, six at primary and five at secondary. From 1960, it became one of the first schools in Hong Kong to offer Mandarin as a third language. The building includes a two-story chapel, a library and other special rooms on the fifth floor, and residential quarters for the friars on the western part of the sixth floor. By 1969, the number of students had reached 4,500. In 1962, the Department of Religion was set up, to provide for the spiritual formation of the Catholic students and religious instruction of non-Catholic ones. During the 1960s, the school set up sports associations and many clubs and social groups. In 1967, the Rosaryhill School Old Students' Association was established. In September 1970, it started a Business Studies program. In 1982, the school was fully subsidized by the government; this resulted in changes to many of the management policies and methods used until that time. The change enabled the school to accept students from more diversified backgrounds and obtain more financial benefits for them. In 1999, the secondary school became co-educational, with boys and girls studying together. In December 2005, a new seven-story annex was opened on the western side of the building, replacing the three-story building that had stood there before. In 2010, the school introduced Spanish language classes at kindergarten, primary and the first three years of secondary school. The students have also performed Spanish music, drama and dancing and prepared Spanish cuisine. Until 2006, the Principal of the Secondary School was a Dominican priest. In September that year, a lay teacher, Francis Tsung Pui-sum (叢培森) became principal, the first Chinese and the first lay person. Since 1959, Dominican priests have managed the school through a Fathers Council, chaired by the Supervisor who is the chief executive of the school. The supervisor since 2018 has been Father Hyacinth He You-sun (何幼孫神父.)

Between 1959 and 1990, there were 826 converts to the Catholic faith among the students, staff and teachers of the school. Its graduates have moved into a wide variety of careers, including the government, finance, teaching, performing arts and social welfare.

Over the last twenty years, the number of students has fallen, in part because of the decreasing birthrate in Hong Kong. Another decision was its designation as a Chinese-medium school in 1998. "I regret it now," said Father Francisco. "I did not fight hard enough for English-medium status. The Cardinal encouraged Catholic supervisors and principals to go for Chinese medium. The Education Department tells us to promote Chinese. But that is not the choice of parents. They moved their children. We have never been a very academic school and could not compete with those with a very high academic standard. We prepare students for the world, to adapt to different situations and countries." It is difficult to manage the language requirements of such a diverse student body in the secondary school. "We cannot force a student into a class in a language he or she does not know." So the secondary school has four classes per level—two, mainly Chinese, who are taught in Cantonese and two, mainly non-Chinese, who are taught in English.

The school building includes a two-story chapel; a library and other special rooms on the fifth floor; and residential quarters for the friars on the western part of the sixth floor. Currently, there are seven priests and seventeen brothers, students and novices.

Its famous alumni include Bernard Charnwut Chan, a member of the Executive Council of Hong Kong; Leslie Cheung, an actor and singer and one of the founders of Cantopop; singer and actress Kelly Chen: actress Kenix Kwok. The Rosaryhill School Old Students Association was established in September 1967 with seventy-five members. Now it has nearly 3,000 registered members. It organizes social gatherings, such as retirement dinners for teachers, sports tournaments with alumni associations, and many volunteer activities.

Dominicans

The Dominicans were founded as a missionary order in 1217 by Dominic de Guzman, a Spanish priest. During the 13th Century, the order spread to France, Italy, Spain, Germany and Scandinavia. In the 15th Century, it sent missionaries to Asia, with the Portuguese Dominicans establishing the headquarters of their mission in Goa, India. In 1587, the first Spanish Dominicans arrived in the Philippines, founding the Province of Our Lady of the Rosary there. Very soon they spread to different Provinces, and in 1611 they founded the University of Santo Tomas, the oldest university in the New World (the Americas and Philippines). In the 17th Century, they went on to Japan and Vietnam, then Taiwan and China. Between 1800 and 1900, the order sent 104 missionaries to China. In 1860, the procuration (headquarters) for missions in China and Vietnam was transferred from Macao to Hong Kong, where it has remained ever since. On July 1, 1861, Father Francisco Rivas opened the Procuration House on Caine Road. From 1907 to 1959, the headquarters was a two-story house in Seymour Road. In 1959, the Procurator moved again, to the St Albert's Priory on 41 Stubbs Road. This became Rosaryhill School. This is a site of 291,500 square feet, which the order acquired in the early 1930s through a public auction. Construction of the Priory began in 1933 and was completed in 1935. Its purpose was to train missionaries. From the beginning, it was international—with Chinese, Taiwanese, Koreans, Filipino, Vietnamese and Spanish studying together. Between 1946 and 1957, the Priory accepted ninety-six members from ten different nationalities; it produced five bishops, seven provincials and four rectors of the University of St Thomas in Manila. But, after the communist revolution, the Order become fearful of the future and decided to set up a new center to train missionaries in Quezon City in the Philippines. This opened in 1958. In 1959, the Priory on Stubbs Road ended its days as a training center and turned into Rosaryhill School. In 2010, the Order opened a novitiate at the school to train people from Asian countries to become priests. Young men have come from South Korea, Japan, Myanmar, Vietnam, East Timor and the Mainland. In 2019, it received fourteen and eight in 2020.

The Procuration house is in Kowloon Tong. That is the home of the Provincial, the head of the Dominican order in Asia.

Like other religious orders, the Dominicans had to decide what to do with Hong Kong's return to China in 1997. "The imminent handover of Hong Kong and Kowloon back to Chinese jurisdiction brought about deep reflection among the friars among the presence of the Order in Hong Kong and the future that lay ahead of them," wrote Eond Eh and Jarvins Sy, both members of the Order, in *History of Catholic Religious Orders and Missionary Congregations in Hong Kong*, published in 2009. "By the late 1980s, faced with the unpredictability of the Hong Kong question, the Province began to diversify their presence in Hong Kong, by assuming ministries outside the educational apostolate of Rosaryhill School, including ministry among the Filipino and expatriate communities, spiritual companionship with diverse religious groups, ministry with the Vietnamese refugees and collaborative work with the different entities of the Diocese."

This was their conclusion about Hong Kong's role in the history of the Order. "It has been the place of residence of the procurator for 145 years. With the establishment of the International Novitiate in Kowloon Tong and a community of postulants in Rosaryhill School, it is presently a key center of formation for candidates to the order in the Asia-Pacific region, where the Province of Our Lady of the Rosary has been ministering for over 400 years. Hong Kong has also been particularly instrumental in the Province's mission in the Philippines, Vietnam and Taiwan.

"Rosaryhill School has been providing education for young people, according to the principles and values of Catholic beliefs, for almost 50 years. It is firmly committed to the formation of the whole human person. In addition, Dominicans are actively cooperating with the diocese in its mission of evangelization and ecumenism," it said. "Given the presence of the order in China, it is hoped that the Dominican mission in Hong Kong will have an important role to play regarding the future relationship between the local Church and the Church in the Mainland."

Juan Jose Morales — Lawyer and Author
In 1996, Juan Jose Morales moved to Hong Kong, armed with a law degree and fluent in several European languages. He became legal adviser to Vita Green, a Hong Kong company that makes health products. He worked with its overseas offices, especially dealing with intellectual property rights. He also opened his own consultancy, Wincomfort Consultants Ltd, specializing in management and trade. "I came here with great enthusiasm and curiosity that has grown ever since. The Hong Kong people are very vibrant. They have much in common with the Spanish — importance of family relations, of food, of large gatherings and of tradition. The culture here is more Chinese than in the Mainland. Hong Kong opened the door for me, through English, to Chinese art, culture and philosophy. I started to collect Chinese art and ceramics. Hong Kong has some of the most important antique dealers in the world. Chinese art include crafts, which have a rich history. In Europe, fine art is more limited, only for the elite." He also developed an appreciation for Japanese art. "Many first-class art historians came through Hong Kong. I learned from them. Hong Kong was also the first bridge of modern Chinese art to the world."

He served as President of the Spanish Chamber of Commerce in Hong Kong and was on the board of several cultural societies, including the Oriental Ceramics Society of Hong Kong. He is Honorary Secretary of the Board of Governors of Musica Viva. He holds a Masters of International and Public Affairs from the University of Hong Kong and studied International Relations at Peking University. He has written widely, including reviews for the *Asian Review of Books* and articles on history, arts and culture in the *South China Morning Post, Caixin, China Daily*, the *Diplomat* and other publications.

He considers his most important book one coauthored with Peter Gordon, *The Silver Way: China, Spanish America and the Birth of Globalization, 1565-1815* (Penguin, 2017). It is a short essay about the discovery of the *tornaviaje* or the return route eastward from Asia to America in 1565, one of the most important navigational feats and discoveries of any time, the Spanish settling in Manila, and subsequent to silver trade between Spanish America and China across the Pacific through the Manila Galleon. This maritime route marked the first chapter in monetary history, with implications for the rest of the world as the silver from Spanish America, and especially the so-called Spanish or Mexican dollar, *Real de a ocho*, became the first world's currency. It heralded the nascence of the first world economy and China's integration in it. The importance of this transpacific silver trade and its worldwide implications were already highlighted by Adam Smith in *The Wealth of Nations* (1776) — but, surprisingly, it all has been forgotten. He co-edited the poetry anthologies *Desde Hong Kong: Poets in Conversation with Octavio Paz* and *Quixotica: Poems East of La Mancha*.

He does not think of retiring, but wants to remain actively working, hopefully more within the cultural world, and always studying. He believes in Hong Kong, still even in bad times better than in many other places in the world. "Hopefully, Hong Kong people can come together to set their own destiny in harmony with their neighbors, in peace and liberty," he said.

Learning Spanish

Historically, Spanish was a minor European language in Hong Kong, with fewer learning it than French or German. But this has changed during the last twenty years. Now thirteen kindergarten and primary schools teach it, as well as twenty-eight secondary schools, half local and half international, and ten universities.

In 2015, the Spanish Ministry of Education signed agreements with two local schools, Rosaryhill School and Law Ting Pong Secondary School, to create Spanish bilingual (Spanish-English) sections. Spanish is used as a medium of instruction at primary and secondary level, along with English, Cantonese, and Mandarin,

In 2017, the Spanish Primary School was founded by Ms Adriana Chan to serve both the local and international communities of Hong Kong, and in particular, the Hispanic community. It is committed to providing a world-class tri-lingual education for them.

In addition, the city has more than twenty commercial language centers and associations where people can take classes. This increase in interest is a result of the rising importance of Spanish in the world and a way for Hong Kong people to do business with Spain and the many countries of Latin America. Globally, 480 million people speak Spanish, making it the second-most widely spoken native language, after Mandarin. Of these, more than fifty million people are in the United States, making it the world's second largest Spanish-speaking country in the world, after Mexico and ahead of Spain. As of 2018, 4,170 people were studying Spanish at universities in Hong Kong, according to the Ministry of Education in Madrid.

Since the colony was founded in 1841, few Spanish people have lived here, other than missionaries. Those who wished to leave Spain for better opportunities abroad could choose one of its many colonies around the world, including the Philippines, a Spanish colony until 1898. Spanish companies mostly did business with this large Spanish-speaking world, rather than China and the Far East. Spain opened its consulate in Hong Kong in 1971, with Enrique Larroque de la Cruz as its first Consul

General.

Father Francisco Miguel de las Heras is a Spanish Dominican who has lived in Hong Kong since 1972 and done much to promote teaching of the language. "There is a lot of interest worldwide in learning Spanish now, more than French. Since 1973/74, I have been involved in teaching Spanish in Hong Kong. In 1962, descendants of Filipinos here set up the Spanish Society of Hong Kong (La Sociedad Hispánica de HK), to create an ambience where their children could practise Spanish. I was invited to their gatherings in the old Repulse Bay Hotel, the Lee Gardens Hotel and the Miranda, three to four times a month. There was also a demand for lessons from British people who had bought retirement homes in Spain. The elderly (Dominican) fathers were in charge of the classes. At that time, the Society was the only place to learn Spanish. The consulate was set up here in 1971. In the early 1990s, private academies opened in Kowloon to teach Spanish. Since the early 2000s, there has been a boom. Now there are many teaching centers in Hong Kong. Since 2012, we have offered intensive Spanish in two classes in our primary school. Now we have ten native Spanish-speaking teachers here. Of the students, 95 percent are Chinese. Their parents are very practical, seeing commercial reasons for their children to learn it, to use in Europe, South America, and the United States."

The Spanish equivalent of Alliance Francaise and Goethe Institut is the Instituto Cervantes (IC). It was established in 1991, under the Ministry of Foreign Affairs and Cooperation, to promote Spanish language and culture, in collaboration with Latin American countries. It has eighty-seven centers in forty-five countries around the world, including collaborations and those that are co-managed. It works with many public and private organizations from Spain, Latin America and other countries to achieve its mission. IC organizes seminars and international conventions; it promotes international cultural networks, has created traditional and online libraries, sets standards for the teaching and professional training of Spanish and accredits people and institutions teaching it.

Although the IC has not yet established a center in Hong Kong, there is a firm commitment by the institution to do so to respond to the demand for learning Spanish. The IC in Beijing and the Education Office of the embassy in Beijing collects information on the study of Spanish in China. According to the latest IC report, 55,816 people in the Mainland are studying Spanish. Of these, 8,874 learn Spanish as part of their primary or secondary studies, or professional training; 34,823 study Spanish at university; and 3,253 were enrolled in one of the IC Centers in the Mainland during the 2017-2018 academic year.

The largest commercial school in the SAR is Spanish World Hong Kong, with more than 800 students. It was founded in late 2005 by a Spanish national, Gonzalo Pérez, with help from two Spanish instructors. Since then, it has taught over 10,000 people. In 2018, it joined other Spanish schools in Singapore and Kuala Lumpur to form the Spanish World Group. It is Asia's largest private Spanish language-learning group, with more than 2,000 students every week. In 2015, it became the only IC-accredited school in Hong Kong and remains so. It offers classes for all ages and levels and a diversity of courses for different purposes. It provides classes at local schools and companies, teacher training programs and use of technology applications as supplementary teaching tools. It has developed a proprietary application that can be used on mobile devices for class management and as a resource for students to learn and practise outside the classroom. It also offers regular workshops on food, wine, music, travel, history, sports and other topics; it organizes events to bring local people close to the cultures of the Spanish-speaking countries.

MARK O'NEILL

The Spanish Chamber of Commerce has taken an active role in the promotion of Spanish in Hong Kong. The Spanish business community was keenly aware that a command of the Spanish language by the local workforce would greatly facilitate commercial exchanges and investments on both sides. By 2001, the Spanish Chamber started to give Spanish language lessons on its premises; it signed the first agreements with local universities to facilitate engagements as trainees of students of Spanish language, among many other promotional activities of Spanish language and culture. This commitment by the Spanish Chamber to promote the Spanish language remains a cornerstone of the work of the Chamber in Hong Kong. Juan Jose Morales served on the board of the Chamber for five years, and was Chairman from 2001 to 2003 (please see his profile in the next chapter).

Two Spanish official exams are available in Hong Kong. One is the Diploma de Español como Lengua Extranjera (DELE). This has been available since 2006, with an exam twice a year, usually in May and November. The other is Servicio Internacional de Evaluación de la Lengua Española (SIELE). It has been available in Hong Kong since 2018. There is no fixed date; the candidate can request and book a suitable time.

Manchu Miguel, cultural officer of the Spanish consulate, said, "The gradual increase in the number of students learning Spanish since 2008 has been mainly due to the inclusion of Spanish as an optional subject in the secondary curriculum. It was incorporated at the initiative of the Spanish Consulate General in Hong Kong, into the Hong Kong government's Education Reform, which came into force in 2008. "Furthermore, in March 2014, the Hong Kong Diploma of Secondary Education was recognized by the General Secretariat of Universities of Spain. This established that students from the Hong Kong educational system (Diploma of Secondary Education or HKDSE) will have access to Spanish universities without the need to take the entrance test. Since then, there has been a significant increase in the number of inquiries about study at Spanish Universities. The support and collaboration of the Hong Kong Bureau of Education, which annually publishes information and access requirements for Spanish primary, secondary and tertiary education, has contributed to this trend.

"There has also been a significant increase in the number of enrollments for the DELE and SIELE exams. Baptist University and the Hong Kong Polytechnic University have recently approved Minor programs in Spanish, in addition to those already established at the Chinese University of Hong Kong and the University of Hong Kong, the latter also with a Bachelor of Art program.

"The Spanish Consulate works closely with local academic and cultural institutions, in particular universities, to promote the Spanish language and culture through the organization of and collaboration in fairs, conferences, and other educational and cultural events. The Consulate awards prizes and provides Spain travel kits to university students of Spanish. For the last twenty years, the Spanish Agency for International Development Cooperation of the Ministry of Foreign Affairs, has sponsored Spanish lecturers — visiting instructors — at two local universities.

"All of this shows the growing presence of and interest in Spanish language and culture in Hong Kong, thanks principally to the enthusiasm and dedication of Spanish teachers. It gives us a solid foundation on which to consolidate and accelerate that growth through the establishment of a sustainable model in Hong Kong, following the IC models in other cities, and of other European academic institutions.

"From our relationship with Spanish learners in Hong Kong, we have learned their principal motives to learn Spanish are professional and cultural, and, of course, for travel. As the second most-spoken language in the world, learners see the opportunity to advance their business and professional prospects in the Spanish-speaking world. At the same time, Spanish is an important language in global culture, for example, in the arts, literature, gastronomy and cinema."

CHAPTER SIX
Two Remarkable Individuals

Hungarian Jesuit World's Top China-Watcher for 30 years
Many priests from Europe devoted their life to Hong Kong and left their mark on the city. One of the most outstanding was Hungarian Jesuit Laszlo Ladany (勞達一神父). He lived in the city for forty-one years. From 1953 to 1982, he wrote and was the sole editor of *China News Analysis* (CNA, 中國消息分析), a weekly and then a fortnightly newsletter. For thirty years, it was the most authoritative account of events in the Mainland, cut off from the world by Mao Zedong (毛澤東). He was the world's most eminent China-watcher. He provided his readers with reliable and meticulous analyses of China's politics, economy, society and culture.

Father Ladany was born on January 14, 1914, in Diosgyor, Hungary. He was the son of a doctor whose original name was Hoffenreich; he was a Hungarian Jew. In 1881, he changed the family name from the Germanic Hoffenreich to the Hungarian Ladany. By 1908, when his father was 31, half of all Hungarian lawyers and doctors were Jewish. That year, like many Jews of the time, his father converted to Christianity. In 1931, the young man entered the University of Budapest; he graduated on June 6, 1935, with a doctorate in law. Also, from 1931 to 1935, he studied the violin under Bela Bartock at the Liszt Music Academy. He initially wanted to become a professional violinist. But he decided to enter the Jesuit Order on July 30, 1936, aged 22. In 1940, he was assigned to the Hungarian Jesuit mission in Taming (大名), Hebei Province (河北省). He went to Beijing for two years of Mandarin study at Chabanel Hall, Shihu hutong (石虎胡同). He gave violin performances at Fu Jen University (輔仁大學) and gatherings of Jesuits. From 1942 to 1943, he taught for two years at a college in Tianjin (天津), followed by four years of theological studies at Xujiahui (徐家匯) in Shanghai (上海). He was ordained a priest on June 8, 1946. In October that year, the People's Liberation Army reached Taming and brought the missionaries in front of People's Courts. Ladany went to Guangzhou (廣州), where he joined Irish Jesuits; they said he spoke English well and Mandarin flawlessly. He began a ministry among university students. The new government expelled foreign missionaries from the Mainland, including the Jesuits. Father Ladany arrived in Hong Kong on June 22 1949 and was appointed chaplain to university students at Ricci Hall (利瑪竇宿舍). He also helped refugees flooding into the city from Guangdong Province (廣東省).

In 1953, the priest who had been his superior in China asked him to write a newsletter to keep the Catholic Church informed about developments in the Mainland. Since Jesuit Matteo Ricci entered Beijing in 1601 at the invitation of Emperor Wanli (萬曆帝), the church had been following closely events in the world's most populous country; to evangelize it had been a mission of the last three and a half centuries. So Father Ladany began what became his life's work or, as some friends put it, "his life". The first issue of CNA appeared on August 25, 1953. For the next thirty years, working out of Ricci Hall, he produced 1,250 issues, a total of 8,750 pages; at first a weekly; it became a fortnightly in January 1979. He was well equipped for the task. He had already spent nine years in China and acquired an excellent understanding of spoken and written Mandarin. He had lived in major cities and rural areas in the Mainland, with and among Chinese people; together with them, he had been through the anti-Japanese and civil wars. He spoke four other languages and had a good understanding of Europe and the Marxism-Leninism that Mao Zedong was introducing. The Church, and the wider world, desperately needed information about the new People's Republic. After Mao sent troops to fight on the Northern side in the Korean War, the western world broke diplomatic relations with Beijing. There were no foreigners in China except for a limited number of Soviet advisers and people from friendly countries, mostly in the communist bloc. There were almost no western journalists or diplomats in China. Mao decided that Westerners had inflicted too much damage on his country; it was time to do without them.

How was the young priest to write his reports? He could not do frontline reporting; few foreigners were granted visas, least of all a missionary from an "imperialist" church. So he began what for the next forty years would become the principal method of Sinology—he read official newspapers and magazines and listened to radios, both central and provincial. They became his basic raw material. This work required a high level of reading and listening to Mandarin, plus the patience of Job to read and listen to material that was often tedious and repetitive and in which the most important news was often expressed indirectly or opaquely, such as through a historical metaphor. Attention to who was in a photograph and who was missing was vital, as was a deep understanding of Marxism-Leninism. He had to know that words and terms do not mean the same in a Marxist country as they do elsewhere. He also interviewed those who had come from the Mainland to Hong Kong. The CNA soon became essential reading for diplomats, researchers, scholars, journalists and business people, in Hong Kong and overseas. They needed to know what was going on in this most important country. The pages described the radical measures and ruthless campaigns that Chairman Mao unleashed on his people.

He was one of the few observers who realized that the Great Leap Forward (大躍進, 1958-62) had caused economic chaos and the greatest famine of the 20th Century. In the CNA issue of August 10, 1962, he reported a massive famine; he used letters sent from the Mainland and accounts by refugees and gave "a realistic estimate" of 50 million deaths. It was one of the first such published accounts. Subsequent descriptions by Chinese and foreign scholars have given similar devastating figures. Father Ladany was one of the few China-watchers to predict the Cultural Revolution (文化大革命). "Almost everyone else first believed that Chairman Mao had everything under control — and later refused to believe the enormity of the cataclysm," wrote Robert Elegant, another famous China scholar and a close friend of Father Ladany.

He also foresaw the conflict between Mao Zedong and Defense Minister Lin Biao (林彪), at a time when the official press presented Lin as Mao's "closest comrade-in-arms". On September 13, 1971, Lin was killed when the Trident he was flying crashed in Ondorkhaan in Mongolia. The official explanation was that Lin and his family had failed in a coup attempt against Mao. This event astonished the China-watching community who could not imagine or explain such a death. But, for Father Ladany, it was no surprise. Even today, nearly fifty years later, we do not know the full story of this key event in Chinese history.

The CNA painted unflattering portraits of communist leaders. These angered admirers of China in the west, of whom there were many in the 1960s and 1970s. But it was impossible to challenge Father Ladany, because his sources were the official Mainland media and he had a prodigious memory and eye for detail.

In 1982, he passed the editorship of the CNA to a team of three young French Jesuit priests. But he did not retire. Instead, he spent the next six years on *The Communist Party of China and Marxism 1921-1985, A Self-Portrait*, published in 1988 by Hoover Institution Press at Stanford University in the US and Christopher Hurst in Britain. "Since it relies entirely on what the Communist Party has revealed about itself, the book is truly, as the subtitle says, "a Self-Portrait of Chinese Communism," Father Ladany wrote in the preface. "Scrutiny of the Chinese sources for thirty-six years develops in the student a sixth sense in sorting out reliable statements from mere propaganda. The Chinese press is not like its Western counterparts. Important events may be kept secret for ten or 20 years ... Many things that happened in the 1950s, even in the 1920s, were not revealed until thirty or sixty years later." That is as true today as in 1987, when he wrote those words.

Despite his encyclopedic knowledge, he remained very modest. This is how his book on the history of the Communist Party begins. "The more you understand China the less you understand her ... The Communist Party is, in essence, a secret society; vital decisions are taken by a few behind closed doors ... After forty years devoted to the study of China and thirty years to the production of a weekly newsletter on China, the

"China News Analysis", I have begun to recognize how much more there is about China that I do not know." Robert Elegant described the Mao described in the book, "The Mao Zedong presented here was not only an ignoramus regarding Marxism but a mean-spirited plotter devoted to his personal safety only a whit less than to his personal advancement. He was also a petty domestic tyrant, as well as a public despot." He said the book was "idiosyncratic, sometimes scathing and sometimes tender, it is unique and quite brilliant."

Father Ladany also wrote *The Catholic Church in China*, published by Freedom House in New York in 1987. It documents many cases of communist persecution of Catholics who did not join the state-sponsored church. They include Bishop Ignatius Kung (龔品梅) of Hankou, who was arrested in 1953 with a large number of Chinese priests on charges of spying. Catholic bishop of Shanghai from 1950 to 2000, he spent thirty years in prison. Another was Bishop Dominic Tang (鄧以明) of Guangzhou, who was arrested in 1958 and kept in prison without trial for twenty-two years. The book showed that Father Ladany did not believe in any genuine religious freedom under the Communist Party. "The difference between the rule of a dictator and communist rule is that, whereas the first uses drastic measures, it rules only over the body. communist rule, on the other hand, is more subtle. It pretends to be democratic, socialist; it holds elections. But it attempts to extend control over the soul of man." He saw China's Catholic Patriotic Association as an instrument of the state to destroy the Church in China.

On September 23, 1990, he died of lung cancer at the Canossa Hospital in Hong Kong, aged seventy-six. He was buried in the St Michael's Catholic Cemetery in Happy Valley. He was deeply engaged in his China studies until he was admitted to hospital a month before his death. One obituary in the Sunday Examiner (

公教報), the official Catholic newspaper, on September 28, 1990, spoke about his humanitarianism as much as his scholarship. "We are not only commemorating his outstanding work and his life, but paying tribute to his heart which really understood, loved and sympathized with the Church in China," said Ho Hoi-ling (何凱玲). "His sense of Justice, experience and solid knowledge of the facts moved him to speak from a sense of justice ... He always said everything without fear of human respect. He worked with dedication and spoke up for the faithful Church in China. His heart beat as one with the faithful Church in China." At his death, he left a completed manuscript, Law and Legality in *China: the Testament of a China-watcher*. It was edited and published in 1992.

The three Jesuit journalists continued Ladany's work but decided that, before the handover, they should leave Hong Kong. In July 1994, they moved to the Socio-Cultural Research Center of Fu Jen Catholic University (天主教輔仁大學) near Taipei, Taiwan, with 900 boxes of archives. The CNA ceased publication in December 1998, after 1,624 issues. The collection of 850,000 articles accumulated since 1953 are now in the Institute of Modern History at Academic Sinica in Taiwan.

Father Ladany always had a dream of a gigantic translation project to make the best Christian literature, from the Church fathers to Nobel Prize winners, available to Chinese intellectuals.

He was a tall, gaunt man who was extremely self-disciplined. He had a sweet-natured Alsatian called Dumbo who was for much of the time his only companion. When she died prematurely, he did not obtain a replacement. He liked to take a swim early in the morning. He smoked a pipe and drank sherry. He lived at Ricci Hall. Initially, he used a motor scooter and then a Volkswagen Beetle. He was fictionalized as 'Father Low', a 'tall handsome Jesuit' in the film *Love is a Many Splendored Thing* by Han Suyin.

Robert Elegant said, "He was a hard man, a very hard man, a man of intense intellectual and moral rigor. He was always hardest on himself. He scorned self-indulgence, however minor or benign. The chief exception to his severe self-discipline was food, which he enjoyed, although he would not permit himself to be a gourmet." John Dolfin, another China specialist and friend of Father Ladany said, "He possessed a deep understanding of Chinese history and culture, the gift of language, the experience of living with and among Chinese people, the intuitive street-smart feel for Chinese political behavior and the comparative perspective made possible by a sound grasp of European social development. In any discussion with Fr Ladany, one always had to be impressed with his razor-sharp memory. He loved being the teacher who kept everyone honest and correct. The value of Fr Ladany's life work will surely not diminish over time, and the memory of his genius will survive as a testament to what can be accomplished in the understanding of a country and civilization as intimidatingly complex as China."

Hong Kong's Swedish son — Anders Nelsson

The media has called Anders Nelsson the Swedish son of Hong Kong. His formative years were spent growing up on a hill above Sha Tin, looking down on villages and paddy fields, long before it was the sprawling 'town' that it is today. His parents were missionaries; Nelsson, who would become a singer, actor, broadcaster and producer, first listened to and fell in love with the rock'n'roll sound of Elvis Presley on the radio when he crept downstairs as a boy during the night at his family home.

In the living room, he says, his father had a radio the size of a cabinet. Long before owning his own set of earphones, Nelsson would place his ear as close to the speaker as he could, so as not to wake up the rest of the family, as he listened to American

EUROPEANS IN HONG KONG

Forces Radio with the latest hits of Little Richard and John Lee Hooker.

"I have the most amazing life," says Nelsson. "I get to do so many different things—music, singing, acting, but all entertainment-related."

"My parents were missionaries and the missionary station compound was in the hills above Sha tin—Tao Fong Shan. It was built in old Chinese style with red pillars. It's Christian but it was intended to attract monks and priests from all different religions from China to come down to Hong Kong, to study one another's religions. So, it had dormitories, a canteen, study rooms, a library—it's still there, it's become more of an ecumenical study center. So, my earliest memories were growing up there."

The Tao Fong Shan Christian Center is situated atop a 130-meter high hill that overlooks Sha Tin and was founded in 1930 by Norwegian missionary Karl Ludwig Reichelt. He asked a Danish architect Johannes Prip-Moller to design the building. Reichelt had previously worked in Hunan Province but came south to Hong Kong to escape the chaos of the Chinese civil war. These days the center is classified as a Grade II historical building.

Nelsson was born in the United States. His Swedish parents moved to Changsha in Hunan Province when he was just one year old where they continued their missionary work; in 1950, they took him to Hong Kong when he was just four years old. Childhood photos of Nelsson show a blond Nordic boy, later as a teenager at King George V School, where he becomes famous in the 60s as the frontman singer for the band the Kontinentals. It was his third band and the one that took off in Hong Kong. And the teenager who did their publicity was fellow KGV student Martin Booth, later the author of, among others, the bestselling *Gweilo* memoir.

"My early years were very rural," says Nelsson. "Previously in Hunan and then above Sha Tin. Then I attended Kowloon Junior School and King George V School, which was much more in the city." After church on Sundays, the Nelsson family would have lunch at the Sha Tin Inn, which is still there today. "We love to stop off there and have satay," he says.

As Nelsson moved into his teens, his love of the music bands of the day grew; he previously told a reporter how he and his friends would all suddenly be trying to talk with Liverpool accents on the playground after the Beatles became popular. But his music foundations are deeper than that.

"It would have started in church, I guess, with my parents being missionaries," he says. "And my mother was very musical and from a musical family. And her older brother heard that his nephew was musical and sent sheet music and records, but, unfortunately, they were too damaged by the time they arrived."

Nelsson's parents would have local leave annually but home leave every five years. Nelsson is trilingual in Cantonese, Swedish and English, but his home has always been Hong Kong, while he would later travel for his music.

The Kontinentals was his third band and the one that took off at a time when Hong Kong was generating a number of home-grown bands during the 60s, including Robert Lee and The Thunderbirds and Teddy Robin and the Playboys. The Kontinentals were the first band from this era to be credited with creating their own songs — often filled with teen angst and fear of rejection, says Nelsson.

They would appear in radio studios and at gigs across Hong Kong and at Hong Kong tea dances where fans in the afternoon would dance the twist, rock'n'roll and do the Watusi.

"They weren't like the concept of British tea dances," says Nelsson — so no string quartet, and delicate porcelain with scones, cream and jam. There would be tea and some simple food, with the more local ones in Yau Ma Tei and farther up Nathan Road serving Pu'er tea with one basket of dim sum of your choice.

Following on from The Kontinentals, Nelsson fronted another successful Hong Kong band Ming, which had record deals and Asian tours. As he hit his thirties, Nelsson was keen to leave singing for a while, entering a new phase of his career — studio production and acting.

Nelsson has enjoyed a series of what he calls walk-on parts in both moves and TV dramas. His most notable perhaps was as a 'baddie' in a fight scene with the legendary Bruce Lee. Nelsson knew Bruce Lee's brother Robert as both of them were in their own bands; he introduced Nelsson to Bruce. The following day, Nelsson turned up at the studio.

"I was one of several baddies in the back streets of Rome," he says. "And I had to attack from behind with a fake lead pipe. Of course, within seconds, his nunchaku sticks had knocked me out."

Nelsson laughs at some of the roles that he has played over the years including a stocks analyst and a professor of vampirology. "I'm brought through a black hole in the universe from the past to assist with a vampire infestation," he explains.

Trilingual in Cantonese, Swedish and English, Nelsson often sings in Cantonese and has nurtured a local fan base. A song about his love of Hong Kong garnered 70,000 likes on Facebook a few years ago. At the age of 60, he decided to return to singing, and this Swedish son of Hong Kong still enjoys performing live.

Conclusion

Ever since Hong Kong was founded as a British colony in 1841, it has attracted people from Europe. It has offered them opportunities for work and professional advancement, higher salaries, a better quality of life and the experience of a society and culture they could not have at home. The only time this stopped was during the two World Wars, when travel from Europe became impossible and the Japanese military occupied the city. After 1945, the process resumed and has continued, throughout the tumultuous changes that have shaken China and the region—the 1949 revolution, the open-door policy and reforms that began in the 1980s, and the handover in 1997. During these 180 years, the role of Hong Kong has remained the same—a bridge between China and the outside world, for people, goods, capital, knowledge, ideas and technology.

In the future, Hong Kong aims to retain this role. It will retain a more liberal visa regime than the Mainland, making it easier for Europeans to come, work and settle. They must provide skills and knowledge needed by Hong Kong and China. As Hong Kong and Chinese people become better educated and more experienced, so Europeans will have to offer skills and specialties not available. They may need a certain level of Mandarin, if not fluency. The attractions of Hong Kong will not diminish—good law and order: civility, good manners and service; excellent public transport; world-class healthcare; tolerance of different races and religions; widespread use of English; diversity and quality of cuisine; sports and social life of many kinds; and easy access to the sea, sailing, swimming and nature.

EUROPEANS IN HONG KONG

China's economy will grow and develop and the number of its foreign residents will increase. So Hong Kong will continue its historic role to support China, in finance, shipping, insurance, aviation, education, the law and other services and as a tourism and retail center. Europeans will be needed in all these sectors. Equally, Hong Kong people will cherish their links with Europe — they will work in European companies, study, work and take holidays in Europe, drink French and Spanish wine and drive German cars. The bonds built over these last 180 years will grow stronger. This book is only the first part of the story.

Sources for this book:

Introduction
Website of EU Office in Hong Kong and Macao.

Chapter One
Dictionary of Hong Kong Biography, edited by May Holdsworth and Christopher Munn, published by Hong Kong University Press.
"German-speaking Community in Hong Kong 1846-1918" by Carl Smith, in Hong Kong Royal Asiatic Society Journal, Volume 34 (1994).
"German Business in Hong Kong before 1914", by Bert Becker, in Hong Kong Royal Asiatic Society Journal, Volume 44 (2004). We thank Professor Becker for revising the text.
"Europe in China" by E.J. Eitel, published by Oxford University Press.
"Arnolds: China Trader" by Vaudine England.
Chu Man Kwong, *International Encyclopedia of World War I*.
Industrial History of Hong Kong, article on "Tai Koo Sugar Refinery" on December 7, 2019.
Website of Evangelical German Community in Hong Kong
On BASF: "Breaking New Ground: the History of BASF in China from 1885 to Today" by Michael Grabicki, published by BASF in 2015.
The websites of BASF and Jebsen & Company.
We thank the BASF office in Hong Kong for revising the text.
Profile of and interview with Hans Michael Jebsen. We thank Jebsen & Co for revising the text.

EUROPEANS IN HONG KONG

Germans in Hong Kong: "Traders of Hong Kong: some Foreign Merchant Houses, 1841-1899" by Solomon Bard, Urban Council 1993.
"The King of Shirts", by Till Freyer, published in 2014.
German Chamber of Commerce, Hong Kong.
We thank Wolfgang Ehmann, Executive Director of German Industry and Commerce Ltd,for revising the text.
We thank Hans Joachim Isler: we thank him for revising the text.

Chapter Two
Hong Kong French Connections, from the 19th Century to the Present Day", published by the French consulate general.
The section on MEP is a summary of the "The Asian Missionary Network of the Paris Foreign Missions" by Bruno Lepeu, in Volume Two of *History of Catholic Religious Orders and Missionary Congregations in Hong Kong*, edited by Louis Ha and Patrick Taveirne, published November 2009.
Archives of the MEP
Website of Sisters of St Paul de Chartres in Hong Kong.
Interview with Paul Clerc-Renaud.
"Wine Industry in Hong Kong," Hong Kong Trade Development Council Research, 17/9/2019.
"Hong Kong is Asia's wine hub," South China Morning Post, 8/11/2018.
Website of HKU-Pasteur Research Pole.
Website of French Consulate General.
Website of WHub.
"Dictionary of Hong Kong", Edited by May Holdsworth and Christopher Munn, Hong Kong University Press.
Le Monde article 20/8/1951.
Paul Clerc-Renaud and Jacques Boissier: we thank them for their precious time and reviewing the text.

Chapter Three

On PIME: "From Milan to Hong Kong, 150 years of mission," by Gianni Criveller, published by Vox Amica Press in 2008. We thank him for his excellent research.

PIME website

Sunday Examiner and 公教報 newspapers.

Canossian Sisters: we thank the Sisters for revising and improving the section on them.

"500 years of Italians in Hong Kong & Macau", an initiative of Consul General Alessandra Schiavo, published in 2013.

Interview with Giovanni Valenti, August 2020.

"Making an Entrance: The Master of the Mandarin", Ernest Kao, *South China Morning Post*, 17 Oct 2013.

"Quality service continues to start back-of-house at historic island landmark", Suzanne Harrison, *South China Morning Post*, 13 Dec 2002.

Chapter Four

"The Portuguese Community in Hong Kong, a Pictorial History" by Antonio M. Pacheco Jorge da Silva, published by Council of Macanese Communities and International Institute of Macao (IIM), published in 2012.

"Making Impressions" by Stuart Braga, also published by IIM in October 2015.

We thank Stuart Braga very much for his excellent research on this topic. We also thank very much Goncalo Cesar de Sa, editor of *Macao* Magazine, who commissioned several articles on the Portuguese of Hong Kong. We have used material from these articles and thank him for allowing us to use the material.

We thank Patrick Rozario for revising the section on Club Lusitano.

Chapter Five

"The Silver Way — China, Spanish America and the Birth of Globalization, 1565-1815" by Peter Gordon and Juan José Morales (Penguin, published 2017).

Interview with Juan Jose Morales, July 2020; we thank him for reviewing the text.

"The Greater Bay Area: to Barcelona and Beyond", an interview with Juan Dedeu, February 19, 2020, on website of Hong Kong Trade Development Council.

Spanish Chamber of Commerce of Hong Kong website.

We thank Father Francisco for reviewing the text.

Chapter Six

China News Analysis, Special Commemorative Issue", November 1990.

Obituary and other articles in *Sunday Examiner* (公教報).

"The Communist Party of China and Marxism 1921-1985, A Self-Portrait" by Father Laszlo Ladany, published by Hurst & Company, London 1988.

Acknowledgements

We thank many people for making this book possible. First, we thank Annemarie Evans for writing several profiles included in the book. This took a great deal of time and energy. Also, we thank all those who gave their precious time for an interview, revising the text and providing various materials. We thank the staff of the French and Spanish consulates: Wolfgang Niedermark, Wolfgang Ehman and Monica Murjani of the German Chamber of Commerce: Pinky Ho, personal assistant to the chairman of the Jebsen Group and Francisco Da Roza. At the end of each chapter, we record the sources for each chapter and those who helped us.

We also thank the directors of Alliance Francaise and the Goethe Institut, Francesco Marascia of the Dante Alighieri Society and Menchu Miguelez, cultural officer of the Consul General of Spain in Hong Kong, for reviewing portions of the manuscript.

About The Author

Mark O'Neill was born to a Northern Irish father and English mother. He was educated at Marlborough College and New College, Oxford. He became a journalist and worked in Washington DC, Manchester and Belfast, before moving to Hong Kong in 1978. There he had the great fortune to marry a Hong Kong lady. He has worked in Asia ever since, working in Taiwan, India, mainland China, Japan and Hong Kong, where he has lived since 2006. He has had the opportunity to meet the rich diversity of Hong Kong residents, both Chinese and foreigners. This book is the result of these interactions. Since 2006, he has concentrated on writing books; this one is his 17th. Earnshaw Books has published three of them, including "Out of Ireland" and "The Island".